Neurolinguistic...

Rhythmic Breath

Ella Adelia Fletcher

07764
936767

MABEL KATZ

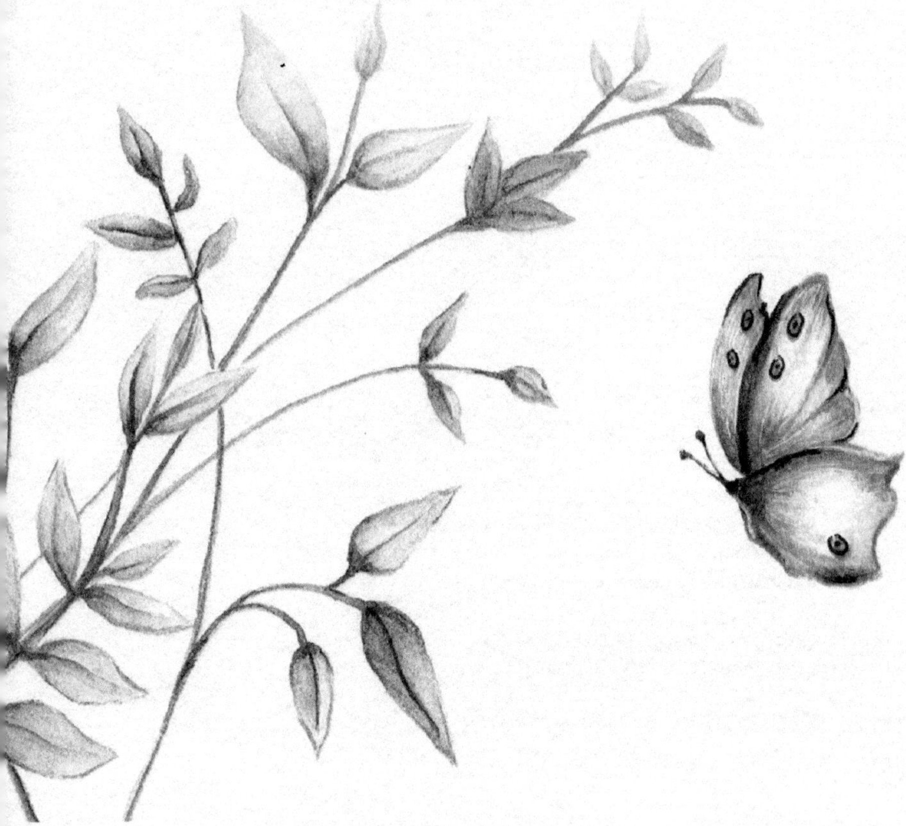

100 Questions about Ho'oponopono

First Edition
Trademarks and registered trademarks are property of their respective owners.
US Copyright Registration Number: TXu002376974

Book Design and Cover Layout by Gladiz Naiza Rosas
Watercolors: Gladiz Naiza Rosas
Translator: Translated from Spanish version Gabriela Rudelir

Publisher's Cataloging-in-Publication data
Title: **100 Questions about Ho'oponopono** / Mabel Katz

Description: Woodland Hills, California | Your Business Press, 2023
Identifiers: ISBN PAPERBACK: 979-8-9866087-1-6
ISBN EBOOK: 979-8-9866087-2-3

Subjects: LCSH: Ho'oponopono. | Self-realization. | Self-actualization (Psychology). | Success - Psychological aspects. | Peace of mind. | Happiness. | Stress management. | Problem-solving. | Self-help techniques. | Spirituality. | Conduct of life.

P.O. Box 427
Woodland Hills, CA 91365
www.MabelKatz.com

PRINTED IN THE UNITED STATES OF AMERICA.

CONTENTS

Message from the Author

I hope you are ready to transform your life and take that next step into your dream life.

Everything you need is within you. You don't depend on anything or anyone outside of you, and in this book, I remind you of that.

Trust your internal GPS. Dare to fly blindfolded. Don't be afraid of fear or uncertainty, you're not alone. The process can be fascinating.

A lot of people tell me that I changed their lives, and hopefully, you choose to be next. Let me accompany you in the process.

Let go and trust.

Mabel

When
we change…
others
change too.

Let Go

and Trust

Introduction

Thank you for
being here
and for giving me
the opportunity
to share
with you...

At these important times of great paradigm shifts, it is key to create a community and cooperate and support each other. Now, more than ever, you must let go and trust and learn to see your challenges differently, knowing that they are always opportunities to grow, learn, and be better.

You must change your perception to see, speak, and act more from inspiration. This is the easiest path to peace, happiness, and abundance.

I know that we are living through difficult times. People write to me from all over the world with fears, worries, and problems, with that feeling that it seems as if the end of the world is approaching. The news sells us situations of fear that makes us live very uneasily and we no longer know who to believe or who to trust, or who is speaking to us with the truth.

You have to realize that we are in a different era. You cannot keep "buying" or getting hooked on certain things. I understand that sometimes it's hard not to, but if you really want to change your life and contribute to creating a better world for yourself and the next generations, you can't keep doing the same things and expect different results. You can no longer afford to keep buying fear because, if you do, you will miss the boat.

It's time to trust and accept that everything that happens is right and perfect. I understand that it is impossible to understand it intellectually, but you can take it further. For that, you have to realize that God (the Universe) is indeed with us, that there is a divine order, and that things don't happen by chance. There is no such thing as good or bad luck: It all depends on your decisions, and it happens because it is right for your evolution and spiritual growth.

I would like to clarify that when I mention God here, I do not do it from a religious point of view. I speak of that part that is within us, that created us, that knows us better than anyone and has all the answers and solutions to our problems. We can define it as a mind more intelligent than ours, which thought about the human body, the mountains, and the oceans.

Let me tell you that I found God within me when I began to trust myself. I do not doubt that we all have Him inside and He is closer than our own breath. He is just waiting for us to give Him permission to act, to protect us, and to guide us in the best possible direction.

Be aware that there is a divine rhythm, you may notice it in nature, in animals or birds. You must recover your rhythm; you are out of tune!

If you can understand a little more, you will possibly be able to accept and perceive what is happening differently. Beyond the cosmos, time, space, and everything that moves and changes, this is the substantial reality, the fundamental truth. This is the real being. Nothing remains, everything changes and evolves; therefore, it is time to remember and connect with that power that we all have. That is the reason why you have to let go and trust. Know that you are not alone and that if you ask for help, the perfect help will always come.

In the following pages of this book, I answer many of the recurring questions I receive. And I'm sure that by reading them you will connect with your own inspiration and receive the answers and messages you are looking for.

It's time to let go of fears and remind you of the power that you have in you, time to wake up and to be able to contribute to this important moment of ascension with your talents and natural gifts.

Time to be aware that you are an embodied, very powerful soul who chose to come to Earth for a purpose and that you have something important to contribute. Yes, you can make a difference in the world.

I invite you to remember what innate talents you have... Your purpose. What would you do to change the world?

Write it here

CHAPTER 1

Let Go and Trust

To attract more miracles
to your life, you must free yourself
from limiting thoughts.

Let go, flow, trust, and be thankful for
what you have instead of focusing
on what you think you lack.

Together let's discover
the answers to your questions.

How do I let go of the past?
How do I change the things I don't like?
How do I delete memories
or the recollections that hurt me?

At some point, we all wonder about these things, and the answer is simple and very important: Decide to change now. Do not wait for the new year or next week to do so. There is always an opportunity to transform ourselves. The time is now. Every breath is a new opportunity; every morning is a new beginning. You don't have to think that the past is something that is going to repeat itself as an endless cycle. It all depends on the choices and decisions you make at any given time.

You must know that God can erase the memories that are stored in your subconscious only if you let go and give permission. That's the only way to stop repeating what doesn't work. Those memories are the ones that continue to choose for you based on what you have lived and make the wrong decisions that control your life without you realizing it.

The only way to start over, or to change your future, is to leave the past behind, to let go of those ancient, even ancestral memories that keep repeating themselves, to start attracting different things.

Every dawn is a new beginning, and every transmuted memory signifies new opportunities.

This is to say that today you can choose to take responsibility, do your best to let go and choose to surrender your problems to God (that part of you who knows best what to do) and give permission to transmute and correct those memories (most from other lifetimes or your ancestors), to be able to act more from inspiration and thus transform your life.

It's about making this a practice until it becomes part of your life. Nayada, from the United States, once asked me how she could let go and trust. So, I explained: This is like exercising, like going to the gym; you have to let go and trust. Unconsciously, it's like breathing as memories are playing all the time. You want to make letting go a habit and a natural part of your life; you want to go with the flow.

I managed to do it, and it really changed my life. When I realized that I was 100% responsible for everything that happened to me, I felt free for the first time. I no longer depended on anyone or anything outside of me. It was one of the things that gave me lots of peace.

Since I was very little, I wanted to be independent, and I felt free for the first time in my life when I found out that everything depended on me. In taking responsibility, I know that everything depends on my decisions. For me, letting go is a new beginning: It is going back to the void (to zero), where anything can happen, where there are infinite possibilities.

If I want a new life, I have to stop living in the past, forgive, and leave behind that heavy suitcase I carry. It doesn't matter what tool

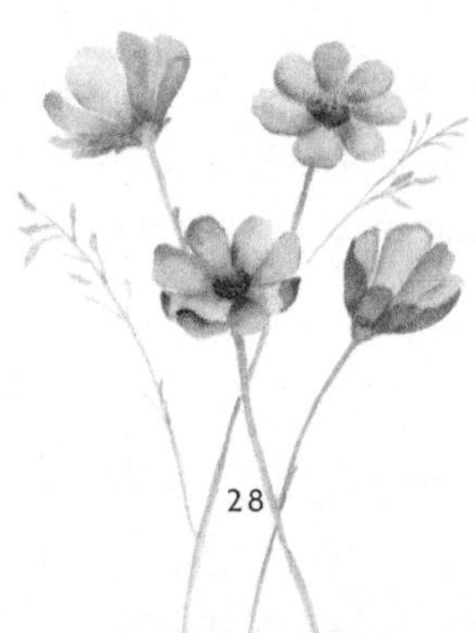

you use or what mechanism works; the secret is to let go of the past and live more in the present.

*I would like to clarify some terms here.
For example, forgiving is not forgetting. Taking responsibility is not a synonym for guilt.
Letting go doesn't mean resignation, and God is not a Being outside of us.*

I also discovered that through the practice and help of Ho'oponopono, I didn't have to worry about all the things that concerned me before. Wow! Can you imagine? From then on, my only concern became asking myself: Am I letting go? Am I permitting God to help me? I share this with you because it works, and because if you practice it, you can also — like me— find that peace and happiness you're looking for. It really works. When you let go instead of worrying, things start to work out in ways you never thought possible.

And yes, let me tell you that sometimes I get hooked, like everyone else. I'm learning like you, but whenever I can, I let go again and try to do it as soon as possible. For example, when a problem arises, if we let go and surrender to God, He knows that He has our permission to intervene and can inspire us with the perfect solution.

Also, something important and that changed my life was knowing that I am not alone, that if I allow it, God will always be there to support me on my path.

Trusting comes with practice, practice, and more practice. You can mentally repeat "I Let go and trust." It's like when you delete something on the computer by accident. If you want different results, you need to change the responses and reactions to the problem. Stop talking to the monitor, expecting for the monitor to change.

I'm reminding you of a wise phrase by Albert Einstein: "Insanity is to continue doing the same, hoping for different results."

How do I know when to take action? And when not to? How to let go and trust, but not fall into passivity?

Many times, there are those people who get confused, and then they ask me: "Well, Mabel, so what do I do? Or how do I make decisions?"

Sometimes it may be that inspiration itself makes us stay at home because, if we went out, we could have an accident, or could avoid an encounter with someone who would cause us a problem. Nothing is a coincidence or an accident. You can choose to start trusting your own inspiration and make decisions by paying more attention to "how you feel" and not "what you "think" is right.

In a chat, a lady asked me if it would be right to move to another country. It was something that made her feel good and she knew it was best for her and her children, but at the same time, she was very afraid. My response was "If this feels good, do it, follow your inspiration. Allow God to guide and inspire you. Pay attention to the signs."

I am always taking action, and making decisions, but also when I am conscious, I am cleaning to allow God to guide me. It is important to be able to stay present, not to worry, to be able to leave everything in God's hands, and to know that it is always better to walk hand in hand.

Many times, you are going to do things because they feel good, and you will think they are the right and perfect one's for you, but you may be criticized or thought of being crazy; therefore, trusting yourself and having faith is very important.

I want to tell you that even if things are right and perfect, or come from inspiration, it does not mean that they will be easy or that there will be no problems. There are always opportunities to correct mistakes, pay off old debts, and break free.

Inspiration will take you where you will be able to learn and thrive and could come to you as a thought, a feeling, a voice, or a sign. It's very personal and different for everyone.

For example, when I answer a question, I'm not thinking, I'm just flowing with it. And this is what you need to work on: You have to stop thinking so much, start acting without thinking, don't plan or at least don't plan too much, become a little more spontaneous, be a child again, and **trust**, **trust**, and **trust** yourself.

Many times you will have to look back to realize that it has been your own inspiration that guided you, and you will say. "*Wow.*" Probably at the moment you will not realize that you are being guided if you stop thinking and analyzing. If you doubt, you lose!

If you're flowing with inspiration, but start questioning, or doubting, you're stopping or cutting the flow. Questions and doubts are also memories, and you can let them go in order to transmute them and thus bring even more inspiration and divine guidance.

You don't need to know or understand. So, this is the idea: Let go, allow your question to be transmuted, and you will see how things start flowing. Many begin to see, hear, or recognize signs. The important thing is that when it starts happening to you, just trust. Do not disregard the signs. Go with the flow.

God will find a way to communicate with each one of us and it will be different for everyone because we are unique. You have to trust yourself. For me, to start trusting represented to work on my self-confidence. Then, I realized that I have something like a magic wand that works only if I let go. Then one day I said to myself, "It seems to me that I'm not alone, and I can choose to give permission to be guided and not have to do it alone." Eureka! I found the easiest way!

What is preventing me from letting go and trusting?

We are all stuck, sometimes more than others; it happens to all of us and perhaps what we need is a reminder to become aware that we need to start by letting go of expectations. What we "expect" is what that part of us that doesn't know anything tells us what we "need" or what we are "missing" to be happy.

When you realize it, you simply have to let go and not engage with that part. Say "Thank you, but I don't have time for this. I have important things to do." You can have many expectations, but you have to realize that it is that part of you talking and making stories as if it knew, and only you can stop it. It is a decision, and it may happen again and again, but we must not give it our power, much less give it control over us.

Deep down, there are always expectations. We all have them. You must manage to let go of them and not allow them to affect you and take you out of the present moment.

Once a video about expectations was shared with me. The following is what I have transcribed for you:

A man came to see God one day:

– "Dear God, may I ask you a question?"

– "Of course, my son."

– "Why did you let so many things happen to me today?"

– "What do you mean?"

– "Well, first, I woke up late and had to hurry to get to work. Then my car took a long time to start."

– "Well..." God said calmly.

– "At lunch, they wrongly made the sandwiches I ordered and had to wait a long time."

– "On the way home, my phone turned off, just as I was getting a call."

– "Okay," God said and smiled.

– "And on top of all that, when I got home, I just wanted to soak my feet in my new foot massager and relax... But it didn't work! Nothing went right today! Why did you do that?"

– God waited until the man finished speaking and then with a smile said:

– "Let me see. The angel of death was in your bed this morning. I had to send one of my angels to fight him for your life. I let you sleep while this was happening. I didn't let your car start because there was a drunk driver on your route. It would have crashed into you if you had been on the road. The first person who made your sandwich today was sick. I didn't want you to catch what he had. I knew you couldn't miss your job. Your phone went out because the caller was going to bear false witness to what you were going to say in that call. I didn't even let you talk to her so you would be covered. And that foot massager had a short circuit that was going to cut off all the lights in your house that night. I thought you wouldn't want to be in the dark."

– "Forgive me, God," said the man as tears began to fall on his cheeks.

– "'Don't apologize, my son. Learn to trust me... in all things, in the good and in the bad. And do not doubt that my plan for your day is always better than yours."

It is important to remember that in the moment, you do not know what is right and perfect for you.

When you become aware that a voice in your head starts telling you stories, you just have to let go but repeating mentally, "Thank you. I love you."

Not buying expectations. By being aware, you can observe them, knowing that it is not you, and not give them power or control.

I know it's hard not to get hooked, and I insist that you don't have to be disappointed if things don't go as you expected, or when not-so-pleasant or painful things happen. Remember you do it to be at peace. It doesn't matter what happens around you. You have to give permission to God to act. He is the only one who can correct things. He helps you find solutions, perceive differently, and regain your power when allowing Him to steer the helm of your ship.

And yes, it is true that sometimes bad things happen, but you do not have to see yourself or others as victims because then you enter into a vicious circle. This is not the way to find the solution you are looking for. The best thing is for you to focus on everything you do have and what works for you. Reflecting on your senses is a true and wonderful gift, such as having two legs that allow you to walk and be independent. And even when your limbs fail you, you have life, intelligence, heart, and hope, which are things that are proven to help you fly through life.

The important thing is to reflect on things you take for granted, that's how it had to be and that's it. How many people are grateful for having two eyes, two legs, and two arms? We don't take it into account; we never give importance or think how blessed and fortunate we are.

So, if you suddenly break a leg, it could be because at some point you didn't listen and didn't take the time to stop. If that ever happened to you, you always have to remember that it could be because something worse was coming, and, above all, if you are practicing Ho'oponopono, you always have to say, "Thank you." Not out of resignation, but out of acceptance that opportunities are coming for you to learn, and we must welcome them. People are always asking "Why did this happen to me?" "I have such bad luck." However, they do not realize that what happened to them is helping them grow, and when we grow, we become better human beings. In addition, as I mentioned above, we will never know what we avoided at the time — that is, what could have really happened. In the same manner, you don't have to hold on to what you're so interested in or want to get. If it is an achievement that you aspire to or something material, you also have to let go and leave it in God's hand by saying to Him: "You know what's right and perfect for me. I will do my part. I let go." We let go of expectations, and we know that, if things don't come the way we expected, it is because something better is coming.

During that time, it is also very important that you open your mind to all possibilities because you never know where the solution may come from. You may be surprised.

For you to let go, you need to stop thinking about it. If you don't let go of the worrying, you somehow are not allowing the right things to come your way. Remember that you have free will, but if you resist it, you don't allow God to act.

You can't be asking outside or comparing because this isn't school. God (the Universe) is watching you, and the more you trust, the more He will look for ways to communicate with you more clearly. He knows you better than anyone else. Trust is a must.

We must also know that we all, at some point, are assailed by doubts. But what to do in situations of doubts and insecurities? The point is that you do not stay hooked or try to understand why this or that happens, or "how" you are going to resolve it. Instead of doing this, you should let go and leave space to receive inspiration. This is a completely different way of seeing the situations in your life. The Universe knows the what's, why's, and how's. You do not have to. You just need to know that there is a memory playing inside your subconscious mind that is attracting your problem and that if you let go, God can transmute it.

Peace is out of our comfort zone, and we often boycott it. This is important! You must be alert at all times to make better decisions. When those memories appear, you say, "Thank you, but I am busy." The important thing is to be patient, keep letting go, and trust your own inspiration. Communicate with God in a way it feels right to you: singing, talking, connecting with nature, dancing: Anything that works for you to stay present and stop the chattering in your head (doubts and fears).

During a seminar in Madrid, somebody asked me: "Does this ever stop?" My response was "Unfortunately, no." This is about learning to become the observer and not engage with it. Live with it and stop giving it the power and control over us. It is about making different choices and decisions. That's where the trick is. Who do we give the power to? Of course, we wouldn't give it to doubts or fears because that would lead us to a vicious circle without getting different results. It is about finding the right answers and solutions by trusting and letting go, and by working with God directly (that part of us that knows better).

Trusting God led me to see greater results. Let me tell you there is no way to do this wrong. We must always do what works for us and trust our own inspiration. Stop listening to the part of you that doesn't know and to others and connect more with your heart.

It gives me a lot of excitement and satisfaction to be able to share this with you and bring a tool that works so that you can be a little more at peace in your life. The road can be difficult, but always keep in mind that there is an easier way. It depends on your choices.

CHAPTER 2

In Search of Our Natural Gifts and the Encounter of Our Spiritual Mission and Journey

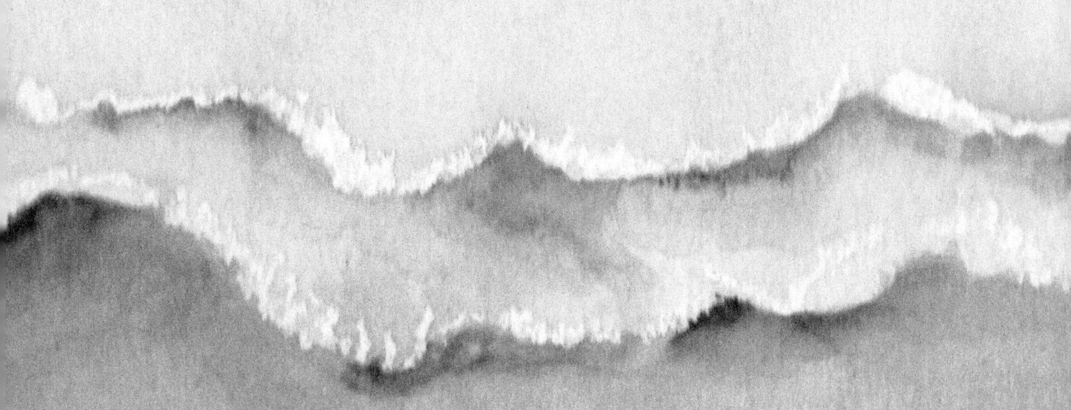

You will never find
happiness
outside of yourself.

When you do what you love,
you are happy, and everything else
will be added.

How do I discover my passion, mission, and spiritual path?

In response to this question, I always respond with what has been a magical question for me: What would you do even if you didn't get paid?

And to answer it, you should never "think" about the response or worry about it. Just respond with the first thing that comes to your mind, even if it sounds ridiculous at the moment. Just go with it. Something will happen and it will come to you spontaneously because there is a part of you that already knows it.

Again, do not be surprised if the answer that arises is ridiculous and does not make sense, nor if there is no answer. You have to keep letting go and trusting that you will discover it at the perfect and right time. You must be patient. When we make the decision that we are ready to know, the Universe takes care of it. But when wanting to find that path, in addition to letting go and delivering, we have to open our minds and be alert because we never know where the answer could come from.

You can naturally talk to God and say, "God, here I am, I'd like to know what my purpose is, what I have come to do on Earth this time."

The important thing is that you feel good about yourself, accept yourself, be grateful for what you have, and live in the present moment. You have to trust, let yourself be guided, and have patience... And, as I have already shared before, I did not immediately leave my career as an accountant. For this to happen, it took several years. I hadn't even contemplated leaving my profession as a tax specialist in the United States.

I can assure you that when you look back, you will be greatly surprised and you will realize that everything was right and perfect the way it was.

When looking for your passion, it is important to pay attention to the signs. Seriously, I did not plan to change my profession. I was happy, I was doing very well, and there was no reason for me to change. I always had plenty of work and made very good money.

But I became a little more aware, a little more open and flexible. I learned to go with the flow. I trusted, and things just started happening on their own. No more planning from my intellect.

Things don't happen by chance, so it's not about having to know what you need, but about letting yourself be guided... Imagine that it was in 1997 when I took my first Ho'oponopono seminar, and anyone would have thought that at that moment I said "Eureka, I found my mission!" But it wasn't like that. I wasn't even looking for it; I thought my professional life worked just fine. I was just looking for more peace and happiness in my personal life.

It wasn't until several years later that I realized this was my purpose. It had never crossed my mind that one day I was going to teach something. I left my profession completely in 2008, and anyone might wonder why so long after my first seminar, but when you look back, you realize that everything was perfect and correct, that it was years of preparation for what was coming.

By the way, my journey with Ho'oponopono began as work for personal growth, and then I began to promote and organize the seminars for my teacher, Dr. Ihaleakalá, and it was always related to my personal life. Yes, I started to practice it as an accountant, and then I realized that it really worked very well in that area too. It was one of the things that helped me trust and believe more in all of this.

Subsequently, I began teaching with Dr. Ihaleakalá, and shortly after, I was already teaching alone, but always as a hobby, on the weekends. Teaching was not my thing.

It is also important to know that many times when you find your purpose, you begin to do it for free, and you start doing it in parallel with other activities. Nothing to worry about or plan. If you allow it, the Universe is going to start opening doors and clearing the way for you.

Important: Please note that even though I tell you that it is important to find out what you would do even if you don't get paid, that is just a clue. That doesn't mean you have to do anything for free for the rest of your life.

On the contrary, there must be an exchange of energy. If we don't pay, we don't receive. If you want to help others, you must charge them, otherwise, the other person will not receive the benefit. We do not value or put in the effort (do our part) when something does not cost us.

Sometimes we want to see results immediately, but God knows what the right and perfect times are for us; we must learn to have a little patience and look within ourselves because that's where everything we are looking for is.

Stay alert. Don't be afraid to be alone or silent. Become the observer. Remember that you are never really alone. Talk to God. He is always there listening to you. Knowing that He accompanies you is also very important because that in itself will give you a lot of peace. Stop thinking and worrying, let go and trust, as everything that is right and perfect for you will come effortlessly.

"Mabel, what can I do to be at peace and be happy?" Good question. The most important thing is to find peace, to be able to be happy, and that is nothing more and nothing less than a decision. When you manage to find that peace and happiness within, everything begins to change and open up. New opportunities will appear in your life, things will begin to happen for you that you will not be able to explain how they happened. That's kind of the idea: first, find yourself so that you can be at peace, feel good in your own skin, free and happy.

If you want to discover your natural talents, let go, trust, and connect with your heart, with the things that are easy for you to do, with those things that do not involve any effort, those that you like to do and give you so much satisfaction, those that you would do for free. The most important thing is to surrender and allow the Universe to show you and guide you. Remember that you have free choice. Don't think or worry. As long as you're choosing to let go and allowing God to transmute those memories playing in your subconscious mind, you're already doing something very important, and you are making a difference because what gets erased from you gets erased from everybody. We are all family.

That's right. Our main purpose is coming to erase and make amends, and that is what we want to do to live more peacefully.

Some people may have come this time with the mission of reconnecting with themselves. They may have come to make a difference in the lives of their relatives, of their community, or maybe just to give birth to a very important soul who will come to make great changes to the planet, or to pay off a debt. Don't get overwhelmed thinking that you must find a mission that makes you famous in the world or become a millionaire. And please, whenever you have an achievement, no matter how small you consider it to be, celebrate it and appreciate it.

A question that many people ask me is, "What do I do with the goals I've set?" Well, if you like to set goals, do not get attached to them because if you are always thinking about them, you'll be living in the future. At the same time, other doors or paths may be opening up for you and you will not recognize them if you are so closed-minded to what you believe is the right path for you. Also, it may not be so bad to let go of your goals, to let yourself be guided, and allow the right and perfect thing for you to only happen in your life as if by magic.

You must be your priority; you have to do what works for you. Be at peace and be happy; don't worry because everything that's right for you is going to come. You must relax, be patient, and treat yourself well. You must practice letting go, trusting, and listening to the heart more in order to be able to identify the things that God has in store for you. It's important to start paying a little more attention to the body, which is wise and intelligent, and ask yourself, "How does this feel? Does it feel good?" Notice your reaction.

In one of our spiritual journeys to Mount Shasta, California, we learned the technique of using the body as a pendulum. Ask a question, and if for example, the body goes forward it means "Yes." It is also called "muscle testing." Some people also use their fingers; if they ask and they open, it means "No." As you can see, you have many tools in case of doubt, without even leaving an inch of your body.

These are not things I use, but there is no doubt that the body is intelligent and knows. This is something I confirmed when I was at the Osho's Ashram once in India, where through very different and interesting meditation techniques I was able to verify that the body is very intelligent. Some included dancing. Others caused our bodies to start shaking and moving. For example, I'll tell you that my body moved on one occasion in a way where I wasn't sure if I was forcing it. When it stopped, I tried to do it again and I couldn't. That showed me that the body can also heal itself because it has that kind of knowledge. We never listen to it because we pay more attention to our intellect and our stories, instead of letting ourselves be guided by this inner wisdom and flow.

I learned to pay more attention to my body, especially my heart, and now I do things because they feel good, not because somebody else thinks that it is the right thing. I learned to stop the intellect, by repeating mentally "I let go and trust," and letting myself be guided, stop the thinking and worrying. And the truth is, that this is what has allowed me to find my mission in life (without really looking for it), and to do things that I've never dreamed of, that would never have occurred to me, and that I did not even learn in school or college.

So pay more attention to your body: how it feels, and whether it resonates with you or not. Don't seek approval on the outside, and don't pay attention to what others think you should be doing or what others expect of you.

If you trust yourself and follow what your heart dictates, you will not get lost and life itself will show you the way.

How do I activate the power of attraction?

What you think, you attract, and once you are aware of the power of your thoughts, you realize the importance of paying attention and working with them, especially those that may be on a subconscious level, that you do not know how they may be playing against what you want to attract.

You are like a *boomerang*. You have to be careful what you do, think, or say because everything comes back. Many times you think things like "I have bad luck," "I am a victim," or "Everyone takes advantage of me."

You're so powerful that you're always right, and if you think like that, that's what you're going to attract. There is definitely a power of attraction and manifestation that we all have innately.

Again I remind you that many of these thoughts may be at the subconscious level and you are not even conscious of them; therefore, it is important to be practicing Ho'oponopono all the time because these thoughts play 24 hours a day in the background.

And if you ever hear yourself repeating any of these phrases, don't engage with them and just mentally repeat "Thank you, but I am busy," or just say "Thank you" or "I love you," and let them go.

You have to let go and trust. The Universe is always there to support you, guide you, and bring you what is right and perfect for you, which, in general, is very near you, but you do not see it, or you cannot identify it because you are not open enough to recognize it.

In the meantime, don't forget to be grateful for what you have. Karla, from Mexico, asked me, "I know I should be thankful for everything I have, but what if I don't like my job?" Even if you don't like the job, remember you are there to clean; it is an opportunity. Do not resist it. Be grateful. Think about all the things you can be grateful for, such as having a job. It's a way to change your energy and give permission to the Universe. If you're not in the right place, don't worry. Something is going to happen, and better doors will open for you. Sometimes you have to close certain doors so that others can be opened. Let go and trust.

Open up and start paying more attention to what is in front of you. You're going to be surprised. Maybe what you are looking for is very close to you. Dare to leave your comfort zone and feel the fears but do it anyway.

"Mabel, how can I attract the right thing for my life?" The best way to attract what is right and perfect for you is to let go and allow

God to guide you; this is the easiest way to do it. You must stop being an obstacle in your own life. You can mentally repeat "I hold God's hand," and thus stop thinking and worrying and live more in the present moment... in the now. The fewer plans you have, the better. I remember that every time I made plans and shared them with Dr. Ihaleakalá, he would tell me that the entire Universe was laughing. Surely you have heard the saying "Man proposes, but God disposes." It is best to live in the present moment and make decisions spontaneously as they come our way.

We must stop complaining and know that everything that comes our way is for our own good. All situations are opportunities to correct and erase, and thus be able to grow and learn. Everything is a stepping stone towards our freedom. That's why you should say thank you for what you like and also for what you don't like. Adversity makes you stronger and a better person.

God will never bring you a situation that you cannot handle. So, you should be proud that God is holding you in such regard. On the other hand, remember that you will always have challenges because life is like that. You are in Earth school! Do you want to graduate, yes? This is your chance!

Things happen to all of us. When a problem goes away, you forget you ever had it, and now you worry because of the new problem you have in front of you. Therefore, you have to know that something is always going to be happening. This is why it is up to you to observe and let go, not to react and resist. Do not identify with the problems and remember that the problem is not the problem: How you react to the problem is the problem. Have you ever noticed that

every time there's a problem you're there? It means that there is something inside you attracting it. This does not make you guilty but makes you responsible, and since it is within you, you can change it, without depending on anything or anyone outside yourself.

On the other hand, please do not identify with those memories of scarcity, nor with the conflicts in the relationships in your life. Just observe them. Most of them are memories replaying from other lifetimes or ancestors. They are all opportunities to erase and set yourself free. You can change them if you are willing to let go and allow them to be erased from your subconscious mind. What is erased in you is erased in others because they are memories in common and appear in your life to give you another chance.

And definitely, Ho'oponopono helps you do that and takes you to zero, to the void, where all the answers and all the solutions are. It helps us to be present and to live moment by moment, not to worry about the future or to get stuck in the past. All we need to do is allow God to transmute in us and inspire us. If we do our part (let go), God does His part (takes care of it).

It is important to be patient because we do not know what is right or what is the perfect time for us. Trusting time! Know that you are not alone and that if you let Him, God is taking care of you, so, when that part of you intrudes and questions —"It seems to me that this does not work,"— you also say, "Thank you" and continue letting go and trusting.

There is not much you have to do; life just guides you if you allow it. "But, Mabel, what do I have to do?" You just have to let go (easier than you think) and let yourself be guided.

As I said before, you surely have special talents and gifts, and you are here for something important. Let the Universe reveal them to you. God already knows what you're looking for. Don't try to push or force anything. Everything comes at the right and perfect time. Let go and trust and prepare to be surprised.

CHAPTER 3

Regaining Control and Power Over Our Life

You will be a victim for the rest of your life if you keep acting as such, and not realize that you have inside of you everything you need to change your life.

How do I adapt to change and stay on track?

God always gives you great opportunities. The issue is whether you're going to react, whether you're going to try to understand it, whether you're going to ask questions that have no answers, or instead just let go and allow yourself to be guided.

Ho'oponopono is "I'm sorry, forgive me for whatever is in me that is attracting this." That doesn't mean you're guilty, and it doesn't make you a bad person or a sinner, but it's only when you take responsibility for everything you do that you can truly make a difference in your life and others.

You need to observe as if you are watching a movie. Remember that the movie is never on the screen, but on the projector. Life is the screen where the memories which are playing in our subconscious are projected.

You are making decisions all the time, and every decision has a consequence. Sometimes you are allowing your replayed memories to choose for you at the subconscious level. But you can choose to make them consciously from inspiration (new information).

If you really want to make a difference in the world, and you want to help, you have to let go, you have to give God permission to correct and inspire you, instead of trying to do it alone, thinking that you know better.

The world has changed a lot. Don't try to understand what is happening. Don't waste your time wondering how you're going to solve things or when you will do it. Just delete what is in your subconscious mind creating all the chaos. Don't miss the opportunity to change it and make a difference for yourself and the world. Remember that Ho'oponopono cleaning is like an investment; it is like depositing money in a spiritual bank that pays very good interest.

Since what is erased in you is also erased in others, especially in your family, relatives, and ancestors, you will never know how many lives you may have saved because we all have common memories. This is why by doing so you stay on the right track; you benefit yourself and you also help others. As I told you, everything comes back. Someone keeps tabs on us.

Do not worry.

If you let go and trust, you will always have what you need when you need it, and you will always be cared for, guided, and protected. Don't get hooked on your worries or fears.

The problems may still be there, perhaps they have not been solved or the fear is not gone; but you must keep going, continue letting go and trusting, and don't let yourself be distracted or controlled by them. The main thing is for you to realize that it doesn't just happen to you. This happens to everyone, and you are simply choosing to be at peace no matter what is going on around you.

The road might get a little harder, but it doesn't have to for you because you go hand in hand with God. You are not alone. Let go of those doubts, those fears, the trying to understand. Always keep looking forward, repeating mentally "I let go and trust," to return to the present moment and move on.

I also invite you to watch my free basic Ho'oponopono course, where you can also learn about the glass of water tool[1] we use to let go and be at peace. Also, some people have reported that it helps them a lot to write and let go of the problem in my Ho'oponopono phone application.

free course
www.mabelkatz.com/freecourse

mobile app
www.mabelkatz.com/app

How do I take 100% responsibility?

I know it can be hard to accept that you're 100% responsible for what you attract in your life. Not only is this true, but it's also very good news. Do you know why? It gives you back your power; it liberates you, and makes you independent.

Please know that when someone tells us a problem, the problem is ours. When a patient tells his pain to the doctor, the problem is in the doctor; the problem is with the teacher, not the student, and so on.

I know this is a difficult concept for the intellect to understand, but they don't come to you or appear in your life because you're guilty, they really come to give you another chance, the chance to erase, and what is erased in you is also erased in them. When you realize this,

1 Referenced on page #125

you stop taking things personally, you let go and surrender, knowing they are allowing you to make amends.

Be grateful for the opportunity, repeating mentally, even if you don't feel it, it's a way to let go and not get engaged. Do not resist. What you resist, persists. This way things start happening, and rewards come faster. You have no idea of God's possibilities. He can have ways to solve your problems and solutions that would never have occurred to you. You have to understand that there is nobody out there taking advantage or abusing you. You are 100% responsible for what you attract in your life, and everything is perfect, just memories replaying in your subconscious mind. Let God accommodate everything, let yourself be guided and, as always, be patient because maybe the solution will not happen overnight... but it will happen.

Many people ask me if by taking 100% responsibility they can set limits or not. And yes, of course, you shouldn't allow yourself to be abused because you are 100% responsible. Sure you can set limits and not accept certain things or people in your life. It is OK to say, "Enough. This is not OK with me anymore," "This doesn't work for me." I can leave an abusive relationship because I love and respect myself and I'm going to set limits, but I will take 100% responsibility. I am responsible; I attracted it. I will not blame the other person, and I will work on myself. Otherwise, I will keep repeating it in other situations or future relationships.

You have to set the limits. If you don't respect yourself, no one will. You can clean with people even at a distance. Again, it is important to remember to take responsibility, to know that you are attracting it, but that does not mean that you should stay there.

By taking 100% responsibility, we also have to keep letting go when things get complicated or do not turn out as we expected, or when we expected. Keep letting go and trusting, accepting, and knowing, in your heart, that God knows best and that there is a divine order. Let go of what makes you unhappy. Don't keep resisting.

Show the other cheek, the cheek of love. Always put yourself first and take care of yourself.

You definitely want to let go of wanting to be right or having the last word. Become humble and realize you don't know what is right. Better choose to be happy, right? Maybe you haven't realized it and there's a reason you stay in toxic relationships or situations, maybe you do it because, unconsciously, there's something about your intellect that considers it positive.

Maybe you have to give up being taken care of, being loved, or being supported. Again, this is just at a subconscious level, that's why you don't realize it consciously. But deep down you're losing much more because you're being dependent on someone else's approval and care. Be aware that you are very capable and can change your life without depending on anything or anyone. You just have to trust yourself. Remember you have everything you need inside.

The idea is to be able to be at peace, but how do you achieve it? You must keep yourself in the present moment and give God permission to take care of you and guide you. Then you will find yourself at the right place, at the perfect time, and with the right people.

"Mabel, but what happens when you have an illness?" We must be grateful even for an illness because it is another possibility to learn, grow, and be better. That illness is your teacher too! We must not take it as if it were punishment or bad luck, nor should we feel bad about ourselves because we did something wrong. You simply have to be grateful, and live moment by moment in the present. It's always a blessing, even if it doesn't look like it. Do not pay attention to your intellect; remember that it does not have all the information and it doesn't know.

Are they all memories in our subconscious mind? Yes, it's all about memories replaying in our subconscious. Even to a headache you want to say, "I love you" and show it the other cheek, the cheek of love. What you resist persists. You can be at peace, even if you have pain or if you are sick. If you relax and are at peace despite having some difficulty, everything will pass faster, it will not be so serious, and it will not bother you so much. Again, if you take responsibility and let go, things will be able to affect you and control you less, plus you will have the universe's help.

Taking 100% responsibility and not worrying often leads to situations where doctors don't understand how a tumor disappeared, how you can continue to live a normal life, how it doesn't hurt anymore, and how you can walk the same... I've heard so many miraculous stories, and sometimes I feel like my life is a miracle too. I know that sometimes it doesn't happen overnight, you have to let go, trust, and be patient.

Fernanda from Argentina asked me: "How do I avoid reacting?" Instead of engaging in a situation, put some distance and become the observer. Do not identify with the problem. Choose to be happy. When you take 100% responsibility and let go, you are more in control of your life, instead of thinking that there is someone outside of yourself who is doing something to you, and you are blaming them for it.

I'll be honest, not everything is black or white. Sometimes inspiration can lead you to take action; other times, it can lead to inaction because at that moment the right thing is to do nothing. The important thing is that you trust your own inspiration, that you do not hesitate, and when things do not change as and when you expected, that you keep letting go, especially of your expectations.

I know that many times you say that you take responsibility, that you let go and you trust, but you really don't. You keep thinking about what worries you, and this is how the process stops because it's like facing two opposing forces: letting go and resisting.

Everything is perfect and correct because the Universe is perfect. Everything happens for some reason that perhaps the intellect will never understand. There are no victims, and we all have what we need inside to get out of those situations. In your case, it all depends on your attitude and your thoughts.

I also have challenges; I also do the best I can. We all do the best we can, and God knows it. These are crucial times. Do not engage on circumstances or events and stop blaming and complaining because each of us has the possibility of erasing those memories in our subconscious. And when you do it, it's a way to make a change and help others too.

When you take responsibility, you're not doing it just for yourself, you're changing the destiny of the world. You're making history, and I swear you're going to be rewarded!

How does the ego affect our energy and how can we free ourselves from it?

What does the ego want? The ego wants to be right and have the last word. It thinks that it knows what is right and perfect, that it knows good and bad, but actually, it doesn't know. It doesn't have the entire information.

On the other hand, it is a very important part of us because it is the part that has the power to choose freely; therefore, it is responsible for initiating the Ho'oponopono cleaning process.

You don't want to resist it or label it "bad" because what you resist persists. It's a matter of making it your ally and showing it that what is better is to be at peace rather than being right.

The ego is, in a way, an illusion, the duality of what we think we are, but it is like part of the game, and we have set the rules before coming to Earth, even if we no longer remember, because precisely forgetting is part of the rules of this game here, on our planet.

That forgetfulness and this world of illusion and duality that we live in is what makes us think that we are something we are not; that's why we are here. We come to remember and reconnect with our true essence.

Many times we criticize and judge because the ego is very strong and all it wants is to be right. It happens to all of us because we give our intellect the power and control to do it. Sometimes we forget that there is no one out there and that everything and everyone is just our memories playing in our subconscious mind. Either way, we keep talking and arguing because we can't help it. I always say that if we didn't talk, we wouldn't have so many problems. As soon as you realize you are engaging, go back to cleaning with Ho'oponopono. Let go. Do the best you can. What you don't have to do is feel bad or guilty. Do not criticize yourself. That doesn't erase. If that happens, as soon as you can, go back to cleaning, letting go, and permitting God to transmute. I remember one of my students telling me that she had done things in the past that she regretted today, but her question was what could she do, apart from asking for forgiveness herself to calm the inner guilt she felt. And my answer was: don't feel bad or guilty if you really want to get over it. Allow God to erase those memories.

Maybe you have to become a little humbler and realize that you don't know as much as you think. That everything happens for a reason. At least for me, it took a very big weight off my shoulders. I no longer needed to know or understand or pretend to be perfect. I just needed to be a little child again and let myself be guided.

And what should you do with your expectations? Another very important change in my life was to realize that expectations were also my ego. That part that thinks it knows how things should be, how Ho'oponopono should work, and so on. And finally, realizing that if I was 100% responsible, it meant that I had created it, that it was within me, and that I could change it myself. I felt free for the

first time in my life. That it depended on me, that my peace wasn't contingent on someone or something changing outside of me.

Maybe this goes against everything you have learned, but you must realize that you have to unlearn to learn again. And please know that the worst thing you can do when you have a problem is to think or worry about it.

You think you're in control, but in reality, you regain control when you relax and let go, and allow that part of you (God) that knows better to inspire you with the perfect solutions and the right answers.

We must be very alert to realize when we are buying our own stories. The reality is that you are like a broken record: Only you can stop it, and nobody else can do it for you.

If you are sufficiently aware of it, you will not want to keep repeating those memories that do not work for you, and you will seek to attract what is right and perfect in an easy way. Don't get hooked. Stop resisting and let go.

CHAPTER 4

Ho'oponopono and Relationships

If you don't forgive,
you are still living in the past.

If you keep living in the past,
you will keep replaying it,
and you will not be able to change
your future.

How can I improve personal relationships?

You have to remember that absolutely all the people who appear in your life do so to allow you to make amends. Amends for what? Memories (errors) from other lifetimes. Yes, you have already been with them in other lives and now they appear in your life playing different roles. That's why I always tell you to observe and not to engage because the real problem has nothing to do with what's happening at the moment; it's all about replayed memories.

So, while relationships will always bring challenges, now you can see them as opportunities to correct, and by not taking them personally, it can be easier to let them pass. You can choose not to react when you disagree with something, or something bothers you. I want you to know that the ideal relationship is not one in which we will never have a "yes" or a "no," or in which we will always agree. The ideal relationship is the one that will allow you to see what it is that is playing in your subconscious mind and that you need to work on. Of course, always remember that you can choose to be happy and at peace instead of imposing your point of view.

Many times, it is not so easy to let go, and on different occasions, you will not be able to avoid it. You're going to be a "snitch." I love it when, in the case of couples or even parents and children, they come to the seminar together and I have the opportunity to recommend that at least one of them stay "sane," keeping their mouth shut and turning on the light in those moments in which the other person gets hooked and is, somehow, in the dark.

You should also know that speaking from the intellect (memories) does not work, no matter what kind of relationship. It doesn't work because you keep repeating memories. It can only work if you allow God to erase first and speak from inspiration, which means that you always have to clean first and let God inspire you with the perfect and correct words, with those that others can hear.

Do not plan or prepare yourself in advance for what you are going to say or what they are going to answer you. Let go and go blank. Stay present. You are there to observe and see what is going to be said. This way you will be inspired by what is right and perfect to say at that moment, not what your intellect thinks is right.

Change your mental conversations and the way you see situations, knowing that every encounter is an opportunity to erase old memories and that others are simply showing you what is playing in your subconscious mind.

You must also remember that you can change, and when you do, everything changes. You don't want to wait for anything to change out there. You don't want to resist. Choose to be happy and at peace rather than to be right.

It is important to accept and respect others point of view, other ways of seeing things. You should know that we do not all see or interpret everything in the same manner because we all perceive differently through our memories.

Thinking is resisting, and speaking is too. So, wait for the moment when inspiration comes. Maybe then you can say something in a way and at a time when others can hear it.

They say that "Silence is golden." Well... try to keep your mouth closed and you will have fewer problems. Besides, we all make mistakes, and we are all here learning. You are too.

A friend once said to me, "Mabel, do you know what I realized? That all the people who appear in our lives are angels.

They appear to give us a chance to correct." And it is so because they are incarnated souls who committed themselves to appear in this lifetime under different roles.

We need to learn to love as God loves us: unconditionally. If we are hurt, we take responsibility and clean knowing that we may be paying off old debts. We want to stay present and stop creating more memories to clean later on. We want to let go of the past and not worry about the future.

We know that all those with whom we disagree are our teachers. In any case, we can repeat mentally to ourselves: "I don't know what I did to him/her in another lifetime, but I'm sorry." And don't be surprised that the relationship changes completely and that you end up having a much more harmonious bond.

How can I improve my relationships with my children?

The first thing you should know is that if you are well, your children will be well.

Children must not see themselves as victims because they are not. Sometimes we carry those crutches with us, which repeat "Because my parents separated when I was a kid..." "Because I come from a dysfunctional family...", "Because they abused me...." We continue to blame others. Excuses! Letting go of the past, moving forward, becoming better people, and thus helping others is just our decision. It's time to grow and take responsibility and permit ourselves to be happy. It's time to know that we deserve to be better and that we don't depend on anyone or anything outside of us to be happy.

Did you realize that in a family all children are different? How could this be? Each of us has different memories, we come to heal and experience different things, and we all have free choices.

It is better to let go and give permission to God: "God, you guide me, you know what is right and perfect for them. I leave them in your hands." I let go and trust.

I know that certain difficult situations can arise with our children, but, again, if we do not know what is right for us, we will not know what is right for them. In those cases, there is no alternative but to ask for help. On several occasions, I had to ask for help. "God, this is a lot for me, I need help." "God, you are asking me for too much, I don't know if I can handle this one." When we do our part (let go), God can do His. Don't try to do it alone.

There will always be things that will get out of hand, but you have to ask God to help you. They can be very difficult situations, such as problems with addictions, prison, children who may be at risk, and so on. It is in such cases, when you know in your heart you can't handle it on your own, when you must ask God for guidance. God will protect and take care of them if you allow it. So, in addition to letting go and trusting, continue to work on yourself.

Allowing God to rescue and care for our children, although it may seem like a comfortable and irresponsible position, is not at all. It is a way to take responsibility, become humble, and realize that we need help.

If you really want the best for your kids, it's very important not to listen to other people's opinions and follow your own heart.

Again, remember that our obligation or work as parents is about being happy. At a conference, I was asked how I did it, not to feel guilty about putting myself first before my children? What you have to keep in mind is that if you are OK, they will be OK. Show them that they have to also do what works for them. Besides, this is the best way to show your children that they do not have to be perfect, and they can be happy too. You are their role model.

Let's teach them to put themselves first, to do what they love, to be themselves, to follow what their heart dictates, and not be guided by what others think of them.

If we love and accept them as they are, they will grow more self-confident and will not be seeking approval from others. They will not be begging for love out there to feel worthwhile. We will be helping them to build strong self-esteem.

The more you keep silent, the less you educate and the more you love them, the more they will fall in love with you. Do not sacrifice yourself for them. Do and give them love, expecting nothing in return. Do it without expectations —"When I'm old they will care for me, they will call me, they will deal with me, they will support me because I sacrificed myself for them." When you sacrifice for them and then you claim and complain, you will likely not get anything of what you expected. On the contrary, you will generate guilt and resentment.

Also, when you raise happy children, they will find their own way and it will be much easier for you.

Now, if for some reason, at some point, there is upset and distance between parents and children, there is no need to worry. Remember is normal. You are together because you have common memories. There will always be memories of other lifetimes playing, ready to be erased. The best thing is to practice Ho'oponopono cleaning, work on yourself, and do not engage with what may be affecting you, which you do not even know what it is, because, as I said, it may be memories replaying from another lifetime. When we do, what is erased in us is erased in them. This is the best way to heal and avoid conflict. When we do that, we do it without expectations and the day you least expect it, the phone or the doorbell will ring, without needing to talk, explain, justify, or anything like that. Total unconditional love.

We leave it in God's hands, we take good care of ourselves, and we observe how things pass, change, and settle.

When memories are replaying, who is going to erase them? Or are we going to leave them for our grandchildren and the next generations? You have to try to observe without engaging, not trying to change anyone. Try to avoid arguing, being right, or convincing others of your point of view. None of that. The happiness or harmony that we are all looking for is not there.

On the other hand, we must remember that attachments and expectations are not good for anyone. Try to fill your heart and soul with spiritual things. That peace you are looking for is inside yourself. You have to try to keep your mind occupied, let go of thoughts, not buy own stories, or get hooked on melodrama. You should say, "Thank you, but I'm busy." Choose to be happy.

Detachment produces great inner peace for us.

I know that as parents we want to help them, we want them happy, we want them well. Of course, we will only do a good job by taking care of ourselves, being happy people ourselves, and showing them by example that there is another way and that they can choose differently, and, in the end, it always depends on the choices they make.

Observe without reacting and do not try to change them, nor tell them what is right or wrong, what they should think, or how they should feel. You can't invade their privacy. You have to become a little more respectful and know that they have their own soul that came to live their own experience. As I said before, which is very important, love them and accept them just they are.

As a young girl, I would have loved to know that I was okay the way I was and that I should always follow my heart. What mattered was what I thought of myself, not what others thought of me. It is also so important that you understand the responsibility that comes with free choice, that everything depends on your decisions, and that decisions have consequences. Nothing depends on others, on the outside, everything is within us. Maybe next time you will think twice when choosing, and by doing so it will change your life for the better.

I'm not telling you not to discipline your children. Of course, we all need limits. The important thing is that they know they are responsible for their own decisions. Let us always give them options, let them know the consequences of their decisions, and let them choose consciously. That way you don't have to be the bad one.

Remember: Instead of arguing, you can mentally repeat "I love you, thank you for being in my life." And it's better to do it when they're sleeping, that way you are talking to their subconscious mind, which never sleeps. Whether they live in your home or not. Don't engage. Choose your battles, some aren't worth it. Don't contradict them, clean! Remember that talking and arguing doesn't work. Don't try to give them advice, don't tell them what's right or wrong, remember that you don't even know what that is, and it didn't work for you either, that it's all about memories replaying. We don't know what we did to them in another lifetime: "Sorry for whatever I did to you, thank you for showing up in my life and giving me another opportunity to correct."

How can I improve my relationship with my partner?

Of course, much of what I already shared about personal, professional, and parent-child relationships applies here as well.

So, as I've already said, it's key to focus on being able to really take responsibility and let go instead of wanting to be right, no matter what kind of relationship we are talking about.

Where should we start to improve relationships with our partners? Let's start by accepting and respecting ourselves because they say that others treat us the way we treat ourselves. So only when we love and respect ourselves, others will be able to love and respect us. Remember that acceptance and respect are very important in any relationship.

And you know what? No matter how many times I repeat things to you and how many times you will read them, every time it will respond to a different need, or you will be ready to receive it differently. We learn everything by repetition (even our names), and no matter how many times we read or listen to it, we all need to keep re-reading and re-listening to be able to change our bad habits. The only way of unlearning is to re-learn again, and this takes practice, practice, practice. And we all need to stay alert because life itself is always trying to get us away from our path. We have to be strong and consistent because the memories in our subconscious mind are powerful and very toxic.

One thing in particular concerning relationships for couples is not to look for them because we feel lonely. In any relationship, when we come from "I need them," it creates codependent relationships. Mental or emotional attachments due to a financial dependency, or status in society, what others think of you, etc., are never going to work for us. Let's not even think that we are going to be happy when we have a partner.

Keep in mind that you can be in a relationship and still feel lonely and empty just the same. Between you and me, the best relationship is the one we could have with God. The one inside us.

You're never going to find what you're looking for outside of yourself. If you believe that, you are fooling yourself.

When it comes to a needy relationship, it is not possible to be completely happy, even if people stay together. Let's work on ourselves first, on feeling good, on needing nobody but God, and knowing that we are not alone. Moment by moment, be OK alone physically and thus be able to be at peace being by yourself. Then, look for a partner, but from "wanting," knowing that you do not "need" it.

The famous expression of "looking for our better half" — as if we are incomplete and we need the other person to be worth it— is an idea, a belief poorly learned from our society, that we keep repeating and makes us very unhappy, but ends up being "programming." And today more than ever we realize that we are programmed for many sayings or ideas like that one. Never accept being in a relationship where you can't be yourself, where you're not accepted as you are, or in a relationship in which you think you are going to change the other person and where you have certain expectations of them.

When you are in a relationship, whether personal, intimate, or professional, no matter what the relationship is, the important thing is to know that you were already together in another lifetime, so take 100% of the responsibility and stop blaming, complaining, and thinking that the problem is the other person. Also, don't wait for the other person to change so that you are happy and at peace. When you change, the other person will change. No one outside of yourself can make you happy.

In relationships, the most important thing is to forgive, let go of the past, and stop hurting ourselves. Remember that it's just memories replaying and that they show up because we are ready to erase, free ourselves, and grow. Memories are very toxic and when they play, they play, and sometimes we cannot help it. We are all doing the best we can. Better to choose to be happy than right.

The point is to live in the present moment. That also gives us a lot of peace in a relationship. Not making so many plans and not thinking so much about the future. Even from a Ho'oponopono point of view, if there is a separation, there's no need to be suffering. Then, observe, let go, ask God to transmute. Remember that the ideal partner will not be one with whom there are no differences or conflicts. Partners will always show us what we have to work on ourselves. There is always some reason why we are together.

God always gives us opportunities. Just remember to be more of an observer, as if you were watching a movie and see that those beings that appear in your life are also doing the best they can and that they are just moved by memories too, the characters in a movie. Nobody does things on purpose, but we can't help it. Those memories are stronger than us, and in Ho'oponopono we recognize the importance of letting them go instead of resisting them.

What about infidelity and abuse? As I mentioned before, I do not say that we must stay in the relationship, and accept betrayal or abuse, but understand that they are also memories and that we must assume our responsibility, understand that they are memories replaying, and the other could not avoid it. Maybe you were the abuser in a prior life. Not everything or everyone is there seeing the way to hurt you. Everyone is living their own movie and weaving their own story.

Every time you feel that tests and challenges are coming your way, remember that you, yourself, have planned it before you came. You wanted to live that experience, you wanted to make amends, and the others are playing the role you asked them to play for you. They are giving you another chance. We are all here correcting, learning, and growing. We need not worry or take things too seriously. God knows what is right and perfect for everyone, and we are here to finally graduate. I don't think you want to have to repeat it, right?

The issue here is, are you going to see yourself as a victim? Are you going to get hooked on your story and the story of others? Are you going to try to understand, when there is nothing that can be understood? Are you going to ask questions that have no answers? Or instead, you are going to let go. Because Ho'oponopono is "I'm sorry, please forgive me for whatever is in me that has created this." Only when you take responsibility you start the path of transformation.

It's about not being attached and enjoying every moment, seeing it as an opportunity and knowing there is a blessing behind each challenge. That everything and everybody in your life is a teacher. A mirror that shows you what is in you. Life is a journey, it is a school, and we are all here learning. So, each one of us has their own lessons and experiences from which to learn, and you can't impose on anyone what you think they should be doing. You have to respect other people's decisions too.

Now, when we clean with Ho'oponopono, we are helping others. Why? because we are letting go and permitting God to erase. What is erased in us is also erased in them.

Don't be surprised if the other person changes or does or says things you would never have expected coming from them. Allow them to change! Don't put people in boxes: "They will never change."

"Always the same." "I told you so." Do not decree it, otherwise, they cannot change because you decided they were not capable of change.

The question is... how do I let go? When things happen, what you need to do is relax, let go, and surrender. And, of course, don't forget to breathe. So, at that moment, you must remember to let go and trust. God will always be there to guide and care for you.

Let go of expectations. You don't know what is right and perfect. When we have expectations, and when we are attached to a certain person, situation, or outcome, we end up being the worst obstacle in our own life, and the only possibility that change happens "out there" is for us to change.

It is important to know that there are definitely no coincidences or accidents. We have memories in common, and we always appear in the lives of others, and they appear in ours to give us that opportunity to correct. The people we are with the most and the ones we live with are the ones with whom we have the most memories in common. The more stuff to clean.

Also, every day, every moment, we have opportunities to let go and trust. Our faith is at stake all the time. The Universe knows what is right for us, for you, and that is what we have to rely on. Simply live moment by moment, in the present, seeing everything as opportunities and not forgetting to thank what we have in front of us. We can always be grateful for our adversities. Now we know they are blessings even if they don't look like it.

Don't resist your opinions and judgments. The key is to simply observe your ego and its reactions. Do not make it wrong. And please do not forget that your emotional part is not you either. It is your subconscious mind, your inner child. So, at those moments you can also reinforce this part of you by telling it: "Everything is going to be fine, we are together, and there is nothing we need to worry about."

You don't have to feel bad about your reactions — it happens to all of us. Do not identify with your anger and resentment. Observe and let go, and you will notice those episodes in your life will be shorter and shorter, and the episodes of love, recognition, and acceptance more lasting. Every time, we want to be more aware and let go faster.

No relationship is easy because most of them are karmic, but anything is possible. Ho'oponopono can help you transform them.

How can I avoid what's toxic in my life and not let myself be defeated by what others will say?

Listening to the heart reminds you that you are not alone. It's as if God speaks to you. That's where inspiration comes to you from. You feel light, powerful, and strong. You realize that anything is possible. It is as if at that moment those toxic and dense memories are melted.

Jorge, from Uruguay, had a difficult relationship with a toxic person in his life. He felt that no matter how much he did on his part, everything always ended very badly. Why was this? Well, we have to know that some negative and toxic people are not worth discussing. We just need to keep our mouths shut and clean. Negativity is the one who will most likely win since toxicity is heavier and denser and could sometimes drag us down. Therefore, we must have the good will to say "No, I do not go there, I do not buy it," and never let ourselves be dominated, imposed on, or allowed to be taken control over us. It is key to choose our peace and happiness above all things.

We must concentrate on doing precisely what we love, what works for us instead of what works for others because doing things for others, putting them first, and sacrificing for them does not work. It doesn't work for us; it will not work for them either.

How do I know when the heart is speaking to me? Ask yourself, "How does this feel?", "Does this work for me?", "Does this make me happy?" Choosing more based on what feels good to you, instead of what is "right" — what makes you feel at peace, not what others think is right. Trusting your gut feelings? Yes.

So next time you have to make a decision, ask your heart, not your mind. Always looking within and connecting with that part of you that knows what is perfect and right for you. If it works for you, it will work for everybody. Always do what works for you, and never try to change others because otherwise, you will accumulate more memories and more blocks in your path.

When we are sure of ourselves, we do not need to convince others. We can even accept and respect the decisions of others. If we are closed-minded, trying to be right and to convince others that what we think is right, we will not be able to communicate well, and the results will be the opposite of what we want to obtain.

Allow the mind to do its thing. Just observe it, but follow your heart, what feels right. Do not confront or try to impose your point of view. This way your heart and mind will be aligned. Let go and choose to be happy. Do not get hooked on your beliefs, opinions, and judgments. Remain observant, putting distance and knowing that you are not those reactions.

Only then you will be at peace, without having to argue or fight battles with others, and you can bring more light to all the situations and circumstances in your life. This way, you would also be working on things that you did not even know were coming, that could have brought much more pain and could have been much more difficult than what you are facing right now, but by letting go of trying to understand, expectations, and the need to be right, by just repeating mentally "Thank you," or "I love you," we trust God because He knows best. That's when incredible things happen, unbelievable solutions, those that some people call miracles.

On the other hand, I want to tell you that with Ho'oponopono, when we talk about forgiving others, we don't need to talk to the other person. What you have to do is forgive in your heart, work on your reaction and those memories that lead you to relive and engage the past in your mind. It is important to decide not to hurt ourselves anymore. Why do we hurt ourselves when we do not forgive? Because we are the ones who take the poison, not the person who does not deserve our forgiveness.

Remember that when we talk about healing and correcting memories of the past (most of them from past lives), it is not something momentary. People will always appear in our lives to give us opportunities to correct, but in our hearts, we must know that we have already been together, and the problems are never those which are occurring in the present, but they are replaying memories. We all have to continue cleaning until our last breath, but it will be easier as long as we don't blame and complain and don't try to understand or justify ourselves. Memories cannot be understood; therefore, we must be prepared to take responsibility and let go. Remember, what is erased in us is erased in others; when we change, others change.

What is the importance of the inner child and how do I ask this part of myself to help?

The inner child is our subconscious mind; it is the one that manages all the functions of our body. Imagine everything that happens in it, moment by moment while we are not conscious, when we do not have to even think about breathing, or how to make our heart beat.

Yes, we are on autopilot: breathing, heartbeat, blood circulation, and so on. Well, your subconscious mind can also do cleaning automatically, 24 hours a day, and that is what we really need because many times we will not be able to avoid engaging and reacting.

This subconscious mind, our inner child, watches us, does not listen to us, just like our biological children do. It is not a matter of talking to them or giving them instructions; the idea is to show them by example. That means we have to do it, we have to start it and commit ourselves, we have to try to do the best we can, to clean as much time as possible so that we can act from inspiration, so that we can attract what is right and perfect for us. This child is going to watch us, and it should be clear that in our "house," when we have a problem, we clean, let go, and hand our problems over to God.

We must practice Ho'oponopono all the time; and if we commit, and practice only one thing, our inner child will be clear and will start doing it for us. Yes, we do have super hero, our inner child, who is the subconscious mind and who can do it for us automatically. To do this, we must avoid confusing that child within us because he needs to be clear about what we do when a problem or challenge arises. This is the part of us that can do it automatically 24 hours a day.

Talking to the inner child is very personal. It can be very different and unique for each one of us; it is like talking to a small child; it is having the certainty that it does exist. For example, in my beginnings, I realized that when I was afraid I would say to my inner child: "We are together, everything will be fine, we give it to God." Immediately afterwards I noticed that I felt more at peace.

Do you have to see it or actually hear it? No. It's just the connection, knowing in your heart that it exists and is watching you.

Another way to talk to it is by saying "We're together, I'm not going to abandon you." If you are going through something difficult that hurts or worries you, tell it "Please let go." Remember that this child is also your emotional part. Other times I would talk to mine and tell it: "This one is too much for us, we give it to God. With this one, we don't even try." Our inner child knows God! The intellect, which is the one that has to choose to let go or not, which is the part of us that initiates the process of Ho'oponopono, it does it blindly. It must trust blindly; however, for our inner child, letting go means peace, it is working directly with God.

Does my inner child look like me when I was young?

The inner child (our subconscious mind), which we refer to here in Ho'oponopono, does not necessarily resemble us. If you can see it, it can appear as yourself as a child, but it can also appear in different shapes or forms, including a flower or an animal. Remember that it is the subconscious mind, a part that was with you in past lives.

It is not in this plane, but it does identify with it, because, as I said before, it manages our body and is our emotional part.

Also, let me tell you that it can change, so don't be surprised, it can have different sex, age, etc.

Talking to the inner child is very personal. It is an individual action, different, and unique for each person. There is no particular formula, but just knowing it exists, acknowledging it, and talking with it, can make a big difference in your results.

As I said, to communicate with it has to be done your unique way. Whatever will work for you naturally. For some people, it may be getting up in the morning, saying hello, telling them what you're going to do that day, and asking or saying, "Could you help me with cleaning when I forget to clean?" Again, this is very personal. You just need to know that it does exist and that it is the best partner you can have in life. And it is important that, if you ask it to please let go, you always do it from love.

You can make it your best friend, with whom you can talk to anywhere, at the market, while you are showering, walking, or doing housework. It is not something for which one has to sit and meditate; it can be done at the same time that we are busy or doing other tasks.

So again, there is no need to do any ritual or ceremony to connect with your inner child. And remember, never compare yourself. You are unique.

It is also valid to sit back, relax and make the connection. You can hug it mentally, thank it, and involve it more in your life. Remember that it's watching you all the time, so trust that it's there with you.

You can reconnect with your inner child at any time and say, "I love you, thank you for being in my life," as you would say to a small child. Nothing more than that. Don't try to convince it that it has to be happy or clean because remember, we always want to come from love and don't give orders.

It is our data bank, which is where all the accumulated memories are. Let's choose not to give power to memories. We must constantly remember that it is very easy to engage with anger, depression, mistrust, expectations, apathy, and sadness. You have to be able to change your narrative. When those thoughts show up, you can always respond: "I don't have the time for that, I have a lot of important things to do. I will not give the power or control to this." It's a moment-to-moment choice because memories are always playing.

The inner child is also our intuition since it is all repetition of memories. Sometimes your child can give you some warnings of something that has already happened and can happen again.

It is also our inner child who can help us connect more with God.

We must remember that every time we say, "thank you," we connect with the inner child because even though the conscious mind starts the cleaning, it has to do the connection with the Source through the subconscious mind (inner child). We don't have to give it instructions, just say "Thank you" and it happens. It's like pressing the delete key on the computer. Do we need to know which are the cables that connect and how the computer actually does the deleting? Not really, the computer already knows how to do it. You just need to press the key. Finally, the subconscious never sleeps, so it can clean while we sleep. Many of our dreams are memories from other lifetimes and, therefore, important moments to clean also.

When people come to the seminars, I always tell them not to worry if they fall asleep because the seminar is actually more for their subconscious mind than for their intellect. Once, Dr. Ihaleakalá took his eldest daughter to a Ho'oponopono seminar with Morrnah Simeona (his teacher), and his daughter slept during the entire seminar, to the point that she snored and Ihaleakalá had to put his hand on her mouth because of the noise. The next day they went to the pool together and her daughter said, "Dad, wait, do you remember what the old lady said? First, you have to clean before you go in." He couldn't believe it because she had slept during the entire seminar!

CHAPTER 5

Ho'oponopono and Health

Illnesses are also memories
playing in our subconscious mind.

You may choose to be at peace,
even if you are sick.

There is always a blessing
behind every challenge.

How could Ho'oponopono help us with illnesses?

What are you focusing on? Are you sure you want to heal? When you notice you start worrying, you have to do your best to let go. What we resist persists. You always have to turn the other cheek, the cheek of love, and know that God is the only one who can heal. This means that God could inspire you to go to the right doctor or get the right treatment. And God could even help you to make it disappear. Depends on your faith. You can always choose to be at peace even if you have pain or you are sick. This way, you are allowing God to act.

Of course, we cannot help but have expectations, but let's remember that this is the intellect that does not know what is right and perfect for us. It could be that, through the disease we are releasing memories. Yes, it could be a gift. An opportunity to heal. Remember that there is always a blessing behind every challenge.

No matter the denomination of the health challenge, is also a memory replaying. The disease may be a way to letting go of old memories. We should always say "thank you," no matter what the condition is or if we don't see improvements.

Diseases are also teachers that are helping us to free ourselves and grow, so, it is important not to engage. To worry and think is to resist, and that brings us to the future and the past. So stay in the present by saying "thank you" to the disease and your body, and that means connecting more with the heart (God) than with your mind.

I'm not saying to ignore a diagnosis or not to follow doctor's orders. What I'm saying is that if you choose to let go instead of worrying, God can surprise you with faster healing or less suffering.

In these cases, it is better to say: "I'm going to let go and trust. I'm going to hand over the sickness (or suffering) to God." It's a way of choosing to be at peace, no matter what. It has to do with trusting, knowing that we are not alone, that everything is perfect, and reminding us that we do not depend on being healthy to be happy or at peace.

We begin to be observant, to live more in the present, and to be more aware. We do not judge, we do not see ourselves as victims, and we know that everything is perfect and that it happens for some reason.

I want you to also keep in mind something important when it comes to diseases, diagnoses, and so on. If you start talking about it and sharing your problem with others, you attract more of the same. You're giving it strength. You don't need other people's compassion. You are not a victim. You just need God and your inner child.

Talking to God and your inner child will relax you, help you release tensions and put aside lots of pressure, and even let go of expectations, and then the problem will pass faster, and you will suffer less. Juana, from the United States, asked me: "Then what do I do if I am actually suffering?" Remember that pain is inevitable, but suffering is optional. You don't have to suffer. That's your choice.

To heal or cure, you must relax because, as you know, just by getting tense many times your head begins to hurt. Just relax and give God permission to intervene, care for you, and guide you. And your inner child must know that you are going to give permission to God, that you are together, that you will not abandon it, and that all will be well.

Beware of that little voice that tells you: "This does not work!" As soon as you hear that, just respond mentally, "Thank you, but I'm busy." Remember that is your intellect talking; that it is from the part of you that does not know much. When we say it doesn't work, it's because we're sorting things out based on little knowledge and expectations. This is the part of us that determines what's nice and what's ugly, what's right and wrong, because it thinks it knows.

We must remember not to give our power away to this part of us and keep letting go and trusting.

Sometimes you have to go through the tunnel before you see the light. Besides, we never know what could have happened if we hadn't cleaned. As I mentioned before, we can't do it with expectations. Our goal is to be at peace no matter what. We don't know what's right for us, much less what's right for others.

Do we choose the illnesses or circumstances of our lives?

If you read the book *The Journey of the Souls: Life between Lives,* by Dr. Michael Newton, you will realize that we, in addition to choosing our parents, also choose many of the circumstances of our lives before coming. This is according to the corrections and amends we want to make from mistakes incurred in other past lives.

Something we must remember is that we do not have to do it alone and that God is always there to help us, but what happens is that we think we are alone, and we are our worst enemy because we choose to think, to worry, and we keep trying to understand and look for solutions outside or from our intellect. Please know that intellects create problems, but do not solve them.

What you have to do is let go. Just say: "God, I give it to you, this is too much for me." When you do your part (let go), God can do His part. You never know where or whom the solution may come from. Open your mind.

Letting go, becoming humble, and surrendering to God always works, but not always as you expect or want; however, later you will realize that the way it turned out was perfect.

Remember that we practice Ho'oponopono to be at peace, no matter what is going on around us. It's about looking at pain, worry, anxiety, or symptoms and seeing them as if they were part of a movie. Knowing that we are watching the screen and that we should not identify with them. The cure is not there.

And it is we who make things worse. This happens when we focus on what doesn't work, resist them, feel powerless, and we see ourselves as victims. And guess what: We are the only ones who can change that. Nobody can do it for us.

Our goal should always be to stay calm and confident. But what if you feel like you're running out of patience? Well, you have to remember that sometimes things don't happen overnight. Practice patience. You can make your condition much better.

If our goal is to be healed, we are boycotting ourselves when we worry, so the best we can do is to let go and give God permission to guide, protect, and care for us.

It is precisely God who is going to help us go through it as well as possible. As with everything, it is an opportunity to erase memories and set ourselves free. The disease can help us wake up too

and realize the power we have inside to turn everything around. Many times, we learn and grow when we manage to overcome those kinds of situations.

Remember that you are not that disease. You are not your body. You are above all your problems. You are the observer. Observe it, but don't identify with it and just repeat mentally: "Thank you, I love you."

Precisely because you are so powerful, you attract what you think. So your goal should be to remain calm. That way you will see that even the anxiety will also dissipate. We will realize that we are returning to our core, that we are fine. We notice that the problem may be there, but we are not reacting to it. It doesn't affect us.

The glass of water tool[2], for example, should help you release those times that are hard to let go. We just need to change the water in the glass as many times as necessary to feel at peace. And when those thoughts and emotions come, try to keep a blank mind and imagine that it is as if you were facing a whiteboard where you see all those thoughts and stories being written. As they show up on the whiteboard, you are going to grab an eraser and erase them.

So, how could we erase those negative thoughts or emotions? You can always use a virtual eraser or a brush with white paint to be able to cover them, so they do not affect you, and you can return to zero faster. We do it as they show up because what we want is for the whiteboard to always be blank – let's not allow anything that gets in the way to take you out of the present moment.

There are many ways to help us in the various situations that we have to face. For example, if there are things that cause insomnia, in addition to helping yourself with breathing, you can help yourself with the whiteboard. The important thing is not to resist

2 *Reference*, *on page #125*

that insomnia either, but to show it the other cheek. Just be open and follow your inspiration coming to you at that moment. You can even get up and start writing at those moments when you cannot sleep and see what comes up. The idea is to be able to be at peace, even if you can't sleep.

At one point, you will not even remember that there was a time you couldn't sleep, that you didn't feel well, or you had excruciating pain, and one day you're going to say, "Oops, do you remember I had that pain, or I had insomnia? I don't even remember when it was gone."

This is exactly what happened to my mom in Argentina. She had very bad pain in her right leg, and one day she realized that she didn't have it anymore and didn't know when it was gone.

As you know, what we attract is what we focus on; so it is best not to think about the problem or the illness all the time. Keep your mind occupied and don't let it control you. Don't be your own obstacle on your path to healing.

Can Ho'oponopono help me lose weight?

I want to ask you not to become obsessed with losing weight and looking thin in order to feel good and be happy. Many times it happens to us that we get what we want, including losing weight, and we realize that we are not happy anyway.

We must understand that we are here because we are worth it, and we have something important to do. We do not depend on our weight to fulfill our purpose in life, and we will be happier if we achieve it than if we lose weight. Actually, the more we accept ourselves the

way we are, and the less pressure we put on ourselves, the faster we will lose weight.

What I ask of you is to put yourself first, to do what you feel is right for you, not what others believe is right. Do not care if others think you are overweight or not. Love yourself as you are. You should know that you are someone important and that there is nothing wrong with you.

I also recommend listening to your body and paying attention to what it asks of you, in addition to talking to your inner child – because the subconscious is your emotional part and the one that can help you handle your physical body. It can definitely help you and is your ideal partner.

As I was telling you, many times we put so much emphasis on a diet, on losing weight, on looking good, and then it turns out that when we adapt to the regime or finally manage to find the diet that works and lose the weight... we still remain unhappy.

Dr. Ihaleakalá used to tell me: "It's not the food that makes you fat. It's your thoughts on the food. If you say something makes you fat, it will make you fat!" This is clearly another proof of the power of our thoughts.

It is likely that if we are happy and accept ourselves as we are, we will not need so much food to be satisfied. Many times the food situation is emotional. It's something we all do. If we are well, maybe the food will not make us fat, or we do not need to eat so much; maybe we will be less hungry. Or maybe, by being happy and letting ourselves be guided, we will find the perfect diet for us!

And speaking of diets, there is one that I share from my own experience, which has to do with my inner child. It happened to me in Japan with some French fries, one of my weaknesses. I ended up throwing them away, and I always talk about how I was able to resist them: talking to my inner child, saying, "We're going to be okay, we can do this, we don't need them, we can be happy even if we don't eat the French fries."

The idea is to become a little child again and not look so much at certain things that you feel are not working the way you expected and want to change to feel better about yourself.

I'm going to repeat it once again because that's what I've discovered about diets: It is very important that we are happy with ourselves and accept ourselves just the way we are. To be thinner, the first step is to dare to be ourselves, love ourselves, and be happy, without depending on anything or anyone. In this case, without depending on how we look. Then, the diet thing becomes a little easier, or the weight is lost faster, but don't put it as "My goal is to lose weight," but "My goal is to accept myself and love myself just the way I am." And, as I told you, it's not about the food, it's about our food thoughts. We all do the best we can. We must always be honest with ourselves. We all have things to clean. Let's just not put weight loss as a goal.

Another very important point is not to put so much pressure on yourself, to be aware that it is not so important. Do I explain myself? We don't depend on our looks to be happy, much less to be someone valuable.

When we reflect on this, we will see that it is actually not that serious. We give too much importance to things that bring us stress and create a lot of pressure when those are not really that important. The really important thing is to enjoy life, just like young children do, and do what's best for ourselves. Sometimes it's just not the right time either...

The key is to be calm because, while analyzing statistics, there are for example people who smoke all their life, who don't take good care of themselves, eat junk food, and they're perfectly fine. On the other hand, others who did take good care of themselves, who did not smoke, and all that, die!

Does it depend on that? Maybe. Of course, we have to take care of ourselves! But beware of your thoughts and emotions. When people went and told Dr. Ihaleakalá that they wanted to quit smoking, his response was: "Why?" Because he explained that as soon as you say, "Smoking is bad for me," you make it wrong and create attachments, and what we resist persists.

Yes, we all have to be conscious about taking care of ourselves but beware of the words we use or the emotions, especially feeling not good enough or bad about ourselves.

Margarita, from Mexico, told me: "Sometimes I'm afraid to say "No" or to set limits." I want you to know that you have the right, and it is OK to put yourself first and set boundaries. Sometimes our illnesses can be due to us not doing the things that work for us because we put others first and we "sacrifice." We are not happy, and we are hurting. Putting yourself first is not being selfish. If it doesn't work for you, you are actually doing a disservice. You are not helping anybody.

We are the ones who should set the limits and we must learn to give ourselves our place, without getting angry or upset. If someone takes advantage of our good will, we must take 100% responsibility because we are attracting it and allowing the abuse.

If it doesn't work for us, it will not work for anybody.

There is something else I would like to address here. If we face difficult situations, we must allow ourselves permission to cry. There's nothing wrong with doing so if it's what we feel we need. This could be a way of setting yourself free too. Do not resist it. You can observe your feelings and remind yourself that you are not your emotions. It may even be a way to release, but the important thing is not to engage and stay there too long thinking we are victims of circumstance, and not give those emotions (memories) the power and control.

I also want to bring up that if you decide to dedicate body and soul to taking care of someone close to you, like a sick parent, do it without expecting anything in return, not even recognition or acknowledgment. It is something that cannot be done out of obligation or guilt. Remember that it can be an opportunity to correct. Maybe that person took care of you in a previous lifetime. Surely a blessing is behind what at the moment seems like an inconvenience. Besides, if this is not right for you, God will send you some help to make it easier on you, or even somebody to replace you so that you can be released from those duties. As always, when you do it from love, when you realize you are there just to make amends, it will always be easier.

Another situation that affects many people happens when they cannot have children. It is another thing that we should not obsess over, and it is necessary to leave it in God's hand, who knows best what is right for us. "God, if I have to get pregnant and have a child, I'm not going to force it, you know what's right for me. If it has to be, it will be, and if not, it is because it is not right for me and there is something better coming, or an important and different purpose that I have to fulfill."

Maybe we had many children in another lifetime, and in this one, we chose not to have them and came into it with a different mission. And if we get pregnant, and we didn't expect it or didn't plan it, we also trust that God knows better. We accept, let go and surrender.

How does Ho'oponopono work in the case of addictions to drugs and alcohol?

The first thing I would like you to be aware of is that thinking is an addiction too, one well-accepted by everyone.

Addictions must be told: "I love you, thank you for being in my life. Thank you for everything you taught me but is time to part. You can leave now. I do not need you anymore." As soon as we label something as bad, we are engaging, which means resisting it, and I don't need to tell you what happens when you resist, right?

If you have somebody in your family (a child, a partner) that has an addiction, every time you notice you are thinking or worrying about it, you can mentally say "I love you, thank you for being in my life." This way you are letting go instead of reacting and you are surrendering the person and the addiction to God, the only one who can help them.

What is erased in us is erased in others. This is the best way to help them, instead of talking to them and lecturing them about what is right and wrong, or what they should be doing.

The most important thing is to let go, take care of yourself, and be happy. Keep busy and do activities that satisfy your soul. If we are well, they will be well. Remember we all have free choice. We all come to live our own experiences, to learn and grow, and of course, to correct mistakes from other lifetimes. Feeling guilty or seeing them as victims doesn't help them. Seeing ourselves as victims doesn't either. We must also realize that if we want to help, it is best to allow God to so.

We, of course, as parents, children, or siblings, suffer and want to help, but the best way to do it is by helping ourselves. If they are part of our lives, it means we share common memories. This is the reason they are in our lives. We have already been together in other lifetimes. There is a reason why they come back this time, to give us one more chance. When we do our part, we benefit, and they benefit too.

One thing we can do is ask God to take care of them and protect them. We hold God's hand. We can tell them that we do not agree with certain things, we can tell them how we feel, but we must respect their decisions, instead of going against them and trying to convince them that the way we think is the right way.

Let them know you care, that you accept and love them as they are, ask them to take good care of themselves, and remind them that they are not alone, that they too can hold God's hand and ask for help.

To oppose is to resist? Yes, and that doesn't help. Of course, the Ho'oponopono

tools can really help a lot here. Even blue solar water can help, when added in drinks and when we cook. Also, blue solar water can be sprayed in the corners of the rooms in the house, especially in those rooms where people with addictions spend more time, where they sleep, etc., because addictions attract entities that could be affecting emotions.

Definitely, we do it without expectations, remembering that we do it to be at peace, no matter what is happening. Even if things change or not, keep trusting and be patient. We can also change the water in the glass, put their photos or names under the glass, etc.

It is important that you always follow your own inspiration.

CHAPTER 6

Prosperity and Money

If instead of complaining and concentrating on what we think we lack, we thank the Universe for what we have, we will always have what we need, when we needed.

How do I let go so that money and abundance flows into my life?

Money is one of the biggest excuses people use for not moving forward in their life and one of the things they are most afraid of.

In my own experience, I have learned that the worst thing we can do is think or worry about it. Not engaging with your limiting thoughts and emotions is the best way to get a good job, attract what you need when you need it, and allow all kinds of abundance into your life.

This has to do with a chapter of my life that I always share because it showed me how God works. I had already quit my accounting and tax practice, and suddenly an income I was counting on disappeared. I already had a big responsibility, which was to pay my employees, and I asked myself: "How am I going to do it alone with this new profession of mine?"

In a way, this was part of a new beginning for me, and I didn't know how I was going to pay salaries now, but, since I decided to let go and leave it in God's hands, I swear it miraculously worked. Of course, I was afraid, and I had anxiety, but I made a decision and said, "God knows why I'm here, and He knows when and how much I need, so… I'm not going to worry."

Whenever worry or anxiety came up, I kept myself as present as I could, repeating mentally "I am not going to worry." This way, I didn't let them control me.

Therefore, I was able to not engage and keep going. It is important not to be afraid of fear. I just noticed the feeling and would repeat, "I'm not going to worry," like a little girl. Let me tell you, I always had what I needed. I didn't have to let anyone go; on the contrary, I had hired more people, and it was not because I had made a budget or a business plan. It was just about letting go and letting myself be guided. The money came from places I couldn't have planned or even imagined, and I just knew in my heart that the money would be there every time I had to pay.

I'm not saying you have to do it just like me: You have to find your own way to stop your concern.

To this day, it is the way I manage my life and my work. I just go with the flow and let myself be guided. When I'm asked about my plans, many times I answer, "I don't know," because the reality is that I do not know and enjoy being able to live moment by moment.

Of course, I know what I have to do. I have to go to South America, the Middle East, or Europe, and I more or less make a plan with the organizers. Buy the tickets so that they are not so expensive at the last minute, etc. I know I will go, but I do not rush to set the dates. The important thing is to flow because things can change when we clean.

Definitely trust is an important part of the formula. When I said, "I'm not going to worry," it was because I trusted God completely, I knew He was the one who was going to take care of it, not me, not my intellect, not my emotions. I knew the latter wouldn't put me on the right track.

There aren't many secrets when it comes to prosperity. It's realizing who we are, that we're not those fears or anxiety, and that we don't have to worry because we're not alone. If you worry, and think that you have to do it alone, and get hooked on those negative thoughts, that's when you get stuck and attract exactly the opposite of what you are looking for.

Many times things are in front of us, and we don't see them. We must remain vigilant. We never know where it's going to come from. We must let ourselves be guided. Doing it alone makes it harder.

You need to trust. God already knows all your needs and responsibility.

It is also important to be grateful for what you have. Focus on the things you possess and not the things you think you're missing. Thanking will change your energy and everything you are attracting.

Say to God, "God, I will do my part (let go) so you can do yours. You know which of my clients, patients, and students are right for me." And remember that you should not worry because God, in addition to knowing all your troubles, knows all your problems, debts, and commitments.

It all starts with us; it is a decision because we have free choice and God does not invade our privacy.

What happens when we get robbed?

Let's start by talking about a special robbery. When we don't love each other, it's like we're stealing from ourselves. Not accepting ourselves as we mean robbing ourselves of the possibility of being happy and at peace. When we don't take responsibility, we rob ourselves of the possibility of being free. We continue to give away our control and power to others.

Someone mentioned to me one day that smoking robbed him of his life, so I think it depends a lot on our perception. I think it's important that you keep this in mind when making your decisions.

What happens when we get our money stolen? Well, it is not right, and I know how that feels, but there's no need to worry because there's a judge who sees it all. Besides, everything comes back in life. So if it was not right, don't worry. We do not have to be the judges and we must not impart justice. And if it was correct because it could have been a debt from another lifetime, and this was a way to pay it back and set ourselves free, it could really be a blessing.

By the way, I want to share with you the story of a young man I met in Los Angeles, who the day he was robbed told the thief: "Thank you for robbing me." Then, the thief began to return everything he had taken from him. He asked him where he lived, and when the young men told him, he was surprised, "That's not a safe neighborhood, let me accompany you." And walked with him as his bodyguard.

Another person in Paraguay told me the same thing, and she ended up going to have a coffee with the thief, whom she insisted that he take her watch, and who in the end did not want to take anything from her.

One thing I want to tell you is that life is like a great theater play, and the program and script are perfect. The robber did not meet the person that was robbed by "accident." It was part of the script. This person may have committed the assault in another lifetime. But of course, at the moment, we would not be able to understand it.

A question that is asked a lot is: What happens in the case of abuse? The same... The victim did not meet that abuser by chance because there is no such thing as chance, but, as we well know, causality. Or, as some say, dissidence. We must understand this. We must wake up and not see ourselves or others as victims. Therefore, do not engage, do not try to understand, and stop blaming and complaining. Let go of the past!

You cannot afford to continue to live in the past. You are hurting yourself and you keep replaying. You are stuck. Your future will repeat itself because you are still living in the past. You must accept, let go, forgive, close the door, and turn the page. Keep seeing yourself as a victim will not allow another door to open. It is also a way to close the doors to prosperity.

Beware that many times we say that we let go, but, in reality, we do not, but we keep worrying, talking, or thinking about the problems. Sometimes we get stuck in situations such as divorces and betrayals. We want justice, but it's also the same issue. We don't know what is "fair" because our memories (debts) from past lives also play a role there.

I know many people wonder what happens when the actions of others hurt us. Well, as I have mentioned, we must not allow resentment and anger to take over and control us. Wish them well, talk to God, and say, "Thank you for the opportunity. You know what is right and perfect."

If at any time it is necessary to take legal action, it is not wrong to do so, but it is important you assume 100% of the responsibility (you attracted it) and letting God direct it and intervene in the process. We let go instead of worrying and let ourselves be guided and protected. That way, the lawyer and the judge, and everyone involved, will also act more from inspiration.

If you wonder why things happen, you should know that everything happens for a reason that the intellect will never understand. They are all opportunities to erase and correct, but please do so without expectations. You want what is right and perfect for everyone involved. Always holding God's hand. He knows what is right for each person, and do not forget to be thankful because what is to come will always be better. Everything is just a blessing in disguise, always for your own good.

Sometimes, because we are looking for a job, we miss the opportunity of starting a business of our own. You must open your mind and be alert. The possibility is there but you will not see it because in your mind, you are "looking for a job." As we always say, we never know where it may come from. Stay alert. Let go and trust.

I understand that sometimes it is difficult to avoid worrying, even a little, but you have to work on it. The key is to know that things happen for a reason, some more difficult than others, but you have to keep letting go and trusting. Be open to miracles. Allow the Universe to surprise you. Things will start happening to you that you will not be able understand or explain how they happened. My experience is that in difficult or scary times, repeating " I let go and trust" or "I'm not going to worry" brings me a lot of peace and produces magical results.

Just do your best. We are all here learning. We need to realize we don't really know; we don't have all the information. We must remain aware and present. Things happen to us, things are done to us, we bend backwards, but with Ho'oponopono, we go back to the center, we go back to zero, we maintain our balance and our connection to Divinity, as much as possible. Nothing to worry about.

How do I get to the road of abundance and stay there?

I'm going to share an experience: the story of the dress for my son's wedding. When I realized that I couldn't wait any longer, that the date was approaching and I couldn't leave it for when I came back from my next tour, I said to myself, "I have to go shopping now." I like things to appear for me, to be guided to them. Besides, I didn't have the time for this, and I didn't feel like spending a lot of money either.

I decided to search the internet and I made a phone call. In addition to having the pressure of being the groom's mom, and wanting to find something special, I was not happy having to invest my time and money in something that I was going to use just once and that is not so important.

When I made that phone call, I spoke to someone who told me that the designer I knew and was looking for was no longer in business, and her dresses were no longer available. She recom-mended a place in Beverly Hills. Of course, I wasn't going to pay the price for that area, but I was curious to see what was in the market and how much one dress like that cost.

Before leaving my house, I spoke to God and the Universe, and I told them: "You already know what I'm going to wear and where that dress is. Please, help me and guide me to find it quickly." I turned on the GPS on my phone because in Los Angeles you always have to use it to avoid traffic and accidents to know what is the fastest route.

Along the way, the GPS showed me that there was a route where I could save three minutes. At another time I would have not paid attention because it was not worth deviating to save only three minutes, but, as I had asked to be guided, I thought that could be a sign.

As I rerouted, on the way, I passed by a very nice shopping center that I practically never go to. To top it off, it was being renovated, and most of the stores were mostly closed or empty. I walked into the only open store. There was no other choice. And there I found the dress! I have to be honest: At one point, I hesitated and even asked if I could return it if I changed my mind, but I immediately said to myself, "Mabel, you asked for help, and now are you going to hesitate?" So from there I went straight home and never drove to the other place I thought I was going.

This is important! You just need to know and be aware of how it works: the Universe is always there for us, even for the not-so-important things, and we can always consult or ask. We don't have to do anything alone, but you have to ask for the help; otherwise it cannot come because you have free choice.

Have you ever heard the story of a man who went to ask the pastor if his fiancée was the perfect woman for him to marry? The pastor replied that yes, she was the perfect person for him. He married her, but, after the wedding, the woman died. It turns out that she had a lot of money and when she passed away, he inherited all her wealth. Now he is angry and goes back to the pastor: "You told me she was the perfect woman for me. I was looking for love, not money." And the pastor replied, "Sure, she was the perfect woman. She came to return the money she owed you from another lifetime. So, she paid it back to you and left."

Interesting, isn't it?

You have to trust that everything happens for a reason, even if you get fired from a job, or if you don't have enough money to pay your debts. Everything is always perfect and correct, and if you let go instead of worrying, everything you need will appear at the moment you need it. Neither before nor after. So please trust because abundance also has a lot to do with having faith.

Dr. Ihaleakalá used to say, "I can't believe that God will put us here and will not give us what we need." Please know that you are not here to suffer.

We must open ourselves to the possibility of setting ourselves free. We need to give permission and just say to God, "I'm ready. I let go. Show me!" And as I said before: If what we want to happen does not happen, it is because it was not right for us and something better is yet to come. We must keep letting go and trusting, and no matter what happens do not worry, so God can take care of it.

How do I practice detachment from material things?

Working on detachment from material things was a very important part of my journey because I realized that I had everything I thought I needed to be happy, but I really wasn't.

A key thing I realized is that I didn't need as much to be happy, and I was even allowed to enjoy things without being the owner. Like, for example, when I met my friend Olga in Switzerland, she handed me the keys to her beautiful big house and told me that I could go whenever I wanted, even if she was not there.

Many people question me about living without goals and without making plans. "And what about our desires and our dreams, Mabel?" they say. It's not about not having them. We may have desires, but we must not be attached to them. We don't depend on fulfilling them to be happy; then we realize that God's desires and plans for us are much better than we could have imagined.

If we stay closed up and determined to get what we want, we may be missing out on something much better. Therefore, I always ask you to be alert, present, and flexible.

Also, plans and goals make us live more in the future, and that doesn't work either. All we have is this present moment. I invite you to stay in the now and open yourself to miracles.

Sometimes, some people have to live certain experiences and learn detachment from things through more tragic events, and natural disasters, such as fires, earthquakes, hurricanes, etc.

When some intense fires occurred in the city of Los Angeles, I saw some videos people recorded, and I wondered "Why did this house burn down and the other just next door, didn't? Could be God's hand there?" Do you understand that, as long as we are "connected" and we are "allowing," we do not have to worry about anything because we will be safe and protected?

We are all here to live our own process. I had to live through the earthquake in Mexico and I have very interesting stories. I learned a lot from it. I think tragedies, earthquakes, fires, and tsunamis are an opportunity for us to wake up because we are still asleep, and we continue to see ourselves as victims.

I will take this opportunity to remind you once again that, when we see people as victims and we pity them, we are not helping them, but the cleaning of Ho'oponopono is about helping us (first) and others. Of course, we are responsible. We are there for a reason. I say to God, "I am sorry for whatever is in me that has caused this, and that does not make me guilty, but responsible." All I can do is let go and surrender, and when I do, I leave God to help them. What is erased in me is erased in others.

And the same thing happens if we see ourselves as victims. We let go and allow God to erase those replayed memories.

Sometimes when we lose everything is when we can see the blessings because that's when we have no choice but to become vulnerable and surrender. Right there, we definitely have no other choice but to detach.

They say wealth is what's left when we lose everything. It is what we have inside: the experiences and the lessons learned.

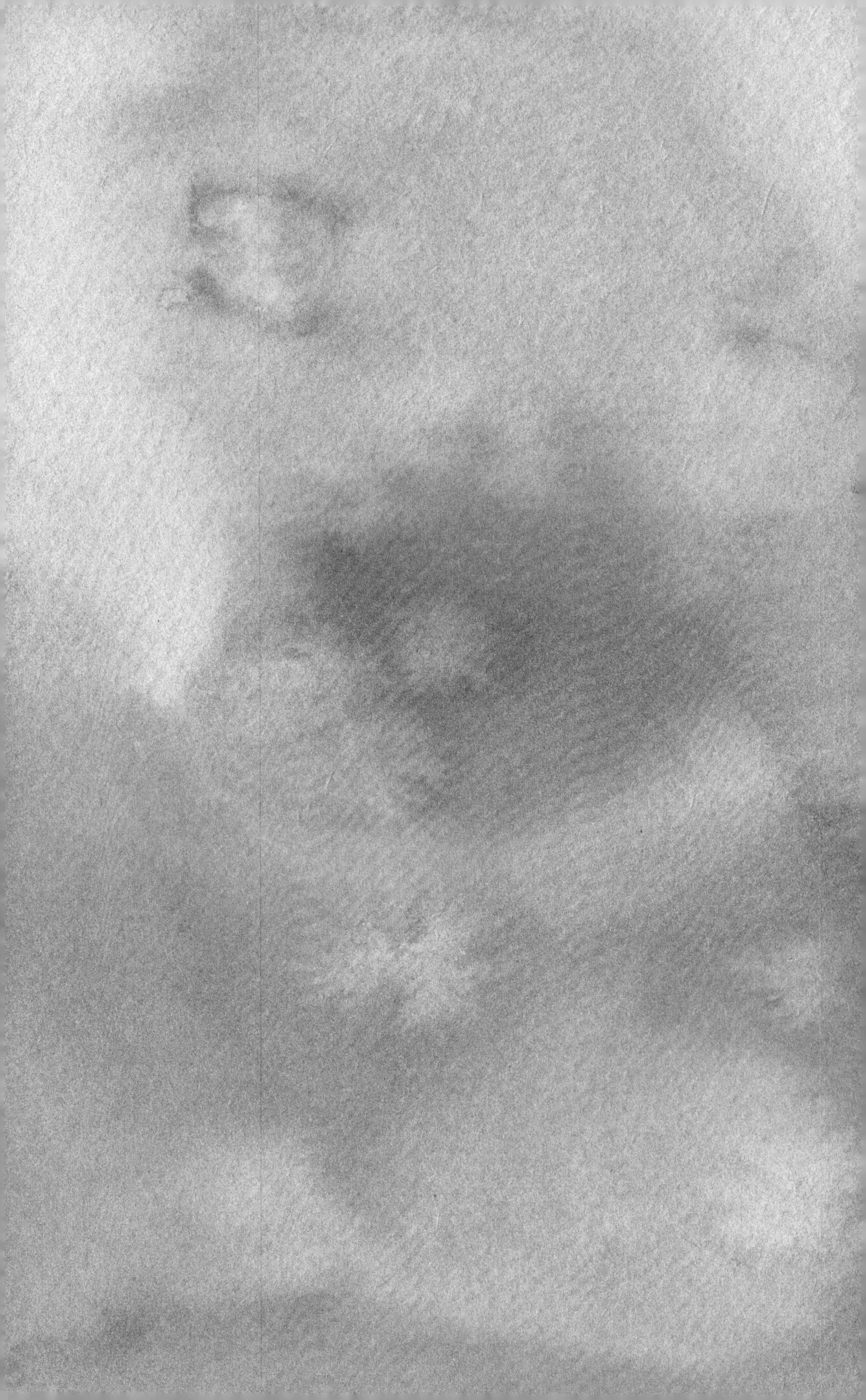

Tools to Practice Ho'oponopono

Gold Ring

Repeating "thank you" or "I love you" is a way of getting protection, but if you feel you need extra protection, mentally repeat "Gold Ring." When you say this, a gold ring will come down (you don't need to visualize it) and Divinity will completely cover you with it.

Remember that you can put the gold ring on other people, but always put it on yourself first.

Vacuum Seal

Another way to get extra protection is mentally repeating "I vacuum sealed myself." It's as if an ice-blue plastic covers you (you don't need to visualize it) and it closes you, just as food it is closed vacuum sealed. You can also vacuum seal other people or objects, but you always come first. For example, I vacuum seal the airplane every time I travel before the plane takes off. Incidentally, this is a tool that was literally taught to me by an airplane during a flight. It may sound a little strange, I know, but it's how I learned this tool.

Glass of Water – Uncovered

- Fill at least 3/4 of a clear or colored glass cup with water from the hose or faucet.
- Change the water a minimum of twice a day, in the morning and night.
- When you feel overwhelmed, you can change the water as many times as you need to feel better.
- You may pour this water into a plant if you feel guilty, but don't worry because your thoughts and emotions harm the world more than throwing a little bit of water away. And if your cat or someone in your household drinks it by mistake, please do not call emergency. Nothing will happen.
- Yes, you can put out more than one glass. Follow your own inspiration.
- You can place the glass at home, at work, or anywhere where you feel inspired.
- The glass of water cleans 24 hours a day. It will clean when you forget to clean.

TIP: You can put photos, legal papers, sheets of paper with names of relatives, friends, addresses, or whatever your inspiration dictates, under the glass of water, only if you feel that it helps you let go and worry less.

Flor de Lis

When I asked Dr. Ihaleakalá about the Flor de Lis tool that had come to me by inspiration while I was in Israel, he replied to the following:

> The Flor-de-Lis is a cleaning process that releases memories of bloodshed, and slavery to ideas, places, situations, and beliefs that result in constant warfare...

The way to use it is "I put the Flor de Lis on the situation."

Later on that same day, he sent me another e-mail saying: "Our minds are stuck in constant warfare with ourselves!" Now I share how to use this tool:

- Mentally you can repeat, "I put the Flor de Lis on the situation."
- This is another way to let go and surrender instead of reacting (resisting).
- It works for all kinds of problems. Follow your own inspiration.

You can join my world peace campaign and help me spread peace and happiness around the world by purchasing at the following link any of the Flor de Lis products that will help you clean 24/7. They will clean when you forget to clean:

www.mabelkatz.com/spreadpeace

Rainbow Lights

This is a tool that Dr. Ihaleakalá gave me to share in my seminars.

- You can mentally repeat at all times (you don't need to visualize), "I wrap the situation in the rainbow lights."
- It works for all types of problems.
- Follow your own inspiration.

The Perfect Cross

This is another tool that Dr. Ihaleakalá gave me to share in my seminars.

- You can mentally repeat at all times (you don't need to visualize), "I put a perfect cross on the situation."
- It works for all types of problems.
- Follow your own inspiration.
- It can be used at all times and for any kind of problem.

"Let Go and Trust"

- At those moments when is hard to let go, where fear and worry are taking over, during those difficult times when you already know that you cannot do much, that you don't know where to run to, or when you are inspired, you can mentally repeat "I let go and trust" like a parrot.
- Repeating this can help you return to the present moment and be more at peace. On some occasions, you will have to repeat it many times to not allow your thoughts or emotions to continue having this power over you and take you on the rollercoaster to the past and to the future.
- It works for all types of problems. Follow your own inspiration.
- It can be used at all times.

"I'm Not Going to Worry"

- You can mentally repeat "I'm not going to worry." It's really a way to hand over your problems to God (the Universe). You are asking for help, and He always listens to you and responds. Let go of expectations and worry by repeating "I'm not going to worry," and go back to the present, moment by moment, so you don't engage or identify with the problem.

- Follow your own inspiration.
- It can be used at all times and for any type of problem.

"Thank You" and "I Love You"

- These are the most famous and well-known Ho'oponopono tools. Remember that you don't have to feel them. The Ho'oponopono tools are like keywords to tell God that we are allowing Him to help.
- It's a way to ask for help and let inspiration guide you.
- You can use them the way you feel: together or apart, in any order.
- Also, don't question who you're telling it to. They're just words.
- You repeat them many times, mentally, at anytime, anywhere, under any circumstances.
- They work for all kinds of problems.
- When you use the tools, you're taking 100% of responsibility (not guilt) and you're handing it over to a part of you that is smarter than your intellect to help you solve the problem the best and faster way possible. All of these replace "I'm sorry, please forgive me for whatever is in me that has created this."
- Always follow your own inspiration.

Glossary

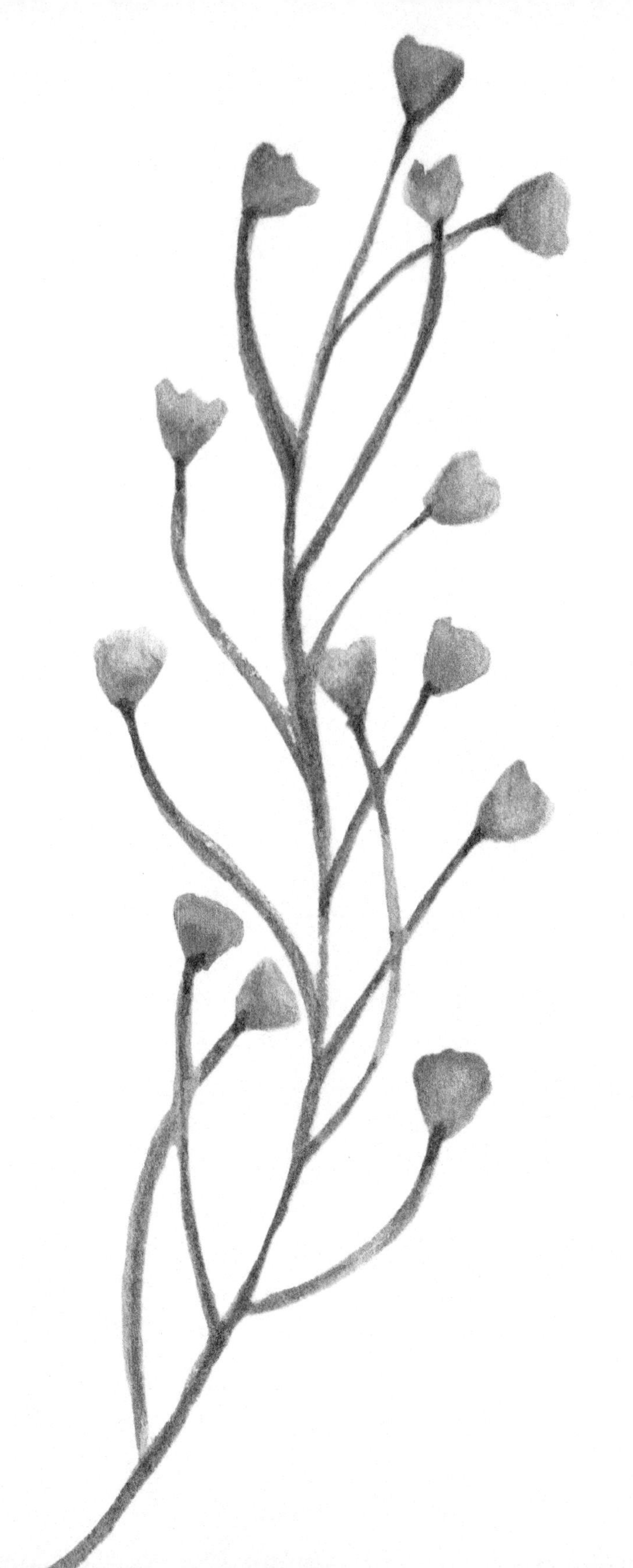

- **Buying:** When I mention "Do not buy it," it means not believing everything we are told, or realizing how we "buy" even our own stories. Many times, it is synonymous with getting hooked or engaging.
- **Codependency**: When we think we depend on things or people to survive financially or to be happy or be at peace.
- **Detachment**: Realizing that we don't depend on things or people to be happy. Accept that everything is right and perfect.
- **Dreams**: They can be from past life experiences or premonitions, things that could happen and we can avoid or prevent. They are all opportunities to clean.
- **Ego**: That part of us that thinks it knows everything. God has given us this part to exercise our free choice, but we have believed that it was given to us to educate us and make us smarter.
- **Forgiveness**: Here I speak of forgiving in our hearts, an inner job to not hurt ourselves anymore and stop living in the past. Also, accept that everything is right and perfect and that there is always a blessing behind every betrayal or deception.
- **God**: When I mention the word God, I'm not, at all, doing it in a religious context. For me, God is that part inside of us that knows everything. Actually, it cannot be defined. It doesn't have a denomination; it's just an experience. It is closer than our own breath. The Universe, nature, an invisible force, a smarter mind than ours.

- **Inner child:** Our subconscious mind, that is, the data bank (where our memories are accumulated). It is the part that manages our physical functions, and it is our emotional part too. It can do the Ho'oponopono 24/7 for us.
- **Inspiration:** New information. It comes from Divinity. It comes to us when we give permission. For example, through Ho'oponopono, by allowing God to transmute what we are ready to let go. This way we're also allowing God to inspire us with the right and perfect answer.
- **Intuition:** Premonitions. They come from the subconscious mind. Our inner child (subconscious mind) can warn us of something that has already happened and is about to happen again.
- **Letting go:** This is handing over our problems to a smarter mind than ours, that created us, that knows us better than anyone else, that has all the solutions and knows what is right and perfect for us. It's a way to surrender, become more humble, and acknowledge that we don't know as much. Do not confuse it with giving up.
- **Memories:** Thoughts, beliefs, decisions, and actions that we have made in this lifetime or previous ones, and that accumulated in our subconscious mind.
- **Memories of other lifetimes:** There is scientific proof that we are not this body, but reincarnated souls. We choose to return so we can make amends from other lifetimes. All these are the memories that we accumulate in our subconscious mind. Remember that we are already born with a lot of information in our subconscious mind (memories), and that some of them could come from ancestors too.
- **100% responsibility:** In Ho'oponopono, we speak of "100% responsibility" as to the programs (memories) accumulated in our subconscious mind, which are the ones that create and are responsible for what we attract in our life. Please do not confuse it with guilt.

- **Programs:** Here we use them interchangeably with the memories we have accumulated, some from this life and many from other lives or even from our ancestors, in many cases, as a consequence of painful events, or decisions, choices, beliefs, opinions, and thoughts.
- **Superconscious:** It is that part of us that is perfect and always connected with Divinity.
- **Surrender:** Become more humble, realizing we don't know a lot. We surrender to a part of us that knows better, and we allow to intervene in our problems, instead of thinking that we can solve them by using our intellect. Please do not confuse it with giving up.
- **Thoughts:** Most of our thoughts are replayed memories.

About the Author

Mabel Katz

Mabel Katz is an author, public speaker, internationally acclaimed world peace ambassador, and leading authority of Ho'oponopono, the ancient Hawaiian art for achieving happiness and peace. She is also the creator of Zero Frequency®, a way of life that teaches 100% responsibility, forgiveness, and gratitude as a pathway to Zero—the state in which we free ourselves from restrictive memories and limiting beliefs so that we may discover our inner talents in pursuit of a more abundant life.

Honored with the prestigious 2012 Mil Milenious de Paz Peace Flag, acknowledging her global peace initiative, **Peace Within Is World Peace,** Mabel was officially recognized as one of the world's pre-eminent peace ambassadors, and on January 1, 2015, was awarded the prestigious Public Peace Prize. She has spoken in front of national senates, and other influential government bodies, including the United Nations in Vienna, where she launched her internationally acclaimed **Peace Begins with Me** campaign. In 2013, she was recognized for her humanitarian works by being knighted in the venerable Order of the Orthodox Knights Hospitaller of St. John – Russian Grand Priory, bestowing upon her the title of **Dame Mabel Katz.**

Mabel continues to travel extensively worldwide, helping countless people find inner peace and greater fulfillment in their lives. She has authored several books, which have been translated into over 20 languages.

When she is not conducting workshops around the world, Mabel brings her unique brand of awareness to prison inmates, special needs children, and dozens of corporate companies seeking to achieve peak performance through deeper self-awareness.

To learn about Mabel Katz' Ho'oponopono and Zero Frequency® Programs addressed to children, parents, and educators — which are a transformational experience — obtain information about her complete line of seminars, workshops, and conferences, or order books, you may contact the author at:

P. O. Box # 427

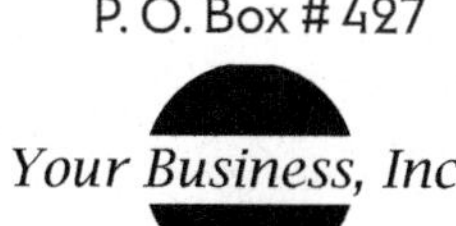

Woodland Hills, CA 91365

Voice mail/Fax: (818) 668-2085

support@mabelkatz.com

www.mabelkatz.com